Facets Of Effective Living

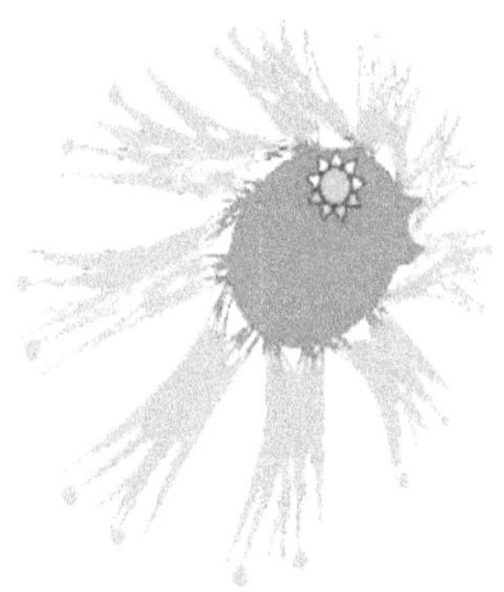

Co-Authored By:

Nawaz Marker   Vinay Kumar   Niranjan Deshpande

Nagesh Babu Maile   Sonia Aggarwal   Kenneth Pinto

Sanjali Ekatpure   Sunita Kulkarnee   Sunita Menon

This book is dedicated to our Mentor

Arfeen Khan

World renowned Peak Performance Strategist, Speaker, Consultant, Coach & Author.

Over 25 years, **Arfeen** has helped over 600,000 people in over 49 countries creating personal and professional metamorphosis.

Arfeen, a magnanimous man with a heart of gold.

We, 9 gems from your treasure chest of coaches thank you for embarking us on this amazing journey of transformation for ourselves and for the world at large.

Nawaz Marker

Vinay Kumar

Niranjan Deshpande

Nagesh Babu Maile

Sonia Aggarwal

Kenneth Pinto

Sanjali Ekatpure

Sunita Kulkarnee

Sunita Menon

CHAPTER 1

Nawaz Marker

Nawaz Marker from Mumbai, is a Confidence & Empowerment Coach, Speaker, Trainer, Networker from past 26 years. She has trained corporate & networkers very efficiently and is an awesome natural public speaker. This is her first published work & now she is an Author.

She is a Science Graduate from Bombay University & has done Systems Management from NIIT. She has years of experience in the corporate sector in Senior Management & her last assignment was Director of Nirmala Niketan

Polytechnic college, where she guided students to 'Live Life at Level 10'.

She is a multi-talented lady, is graceful and an energetic dancer. She has done creative work like stained glass, metal embossing, ceramics, mural, art works, etc.

She is passionately a people's person having a beautiful relationship with her husband, an awesome mother of a wonderful daughter and doting on her grandson and granddaughter. She is a Woman of Substance.

Her mission is to reach out to people and help them transform their mindset and empower their lives with confidence & self-esteem.

STAY CONFIDENT BE EMPOWERED

As I stood there, so happy to return to this pond again, the rain drops making ripples of water.......so rightly did she say, the centre is you, and your thoughts create the ripples.........and cripple you!

Drop a pebble in the pond and see the ripples they form .....

The emotion that creates waves of joy or that of grief, remorse.....

In any disturbing situation do thoughts like the following form ripples in your mind?

-Why can't I speak up?

-Why do words get stuck on my lips and I can't open my mouth?

-Will I ever be able to speak up for myself?

-I do my work well. Then why can't I speak when the time is right?

-What happens to me? Why can't I give back when I am accused wrongly?

It wasn't even my mistake and I got choked.......

-I have done such good work and forgotten just one thing. Yet my boss keeps harping on that. What can I do?

-Why do such bad things happen to me only?

-Am I good enough?

-Can I do it?

-Why do I feel this deep pain and not able to take a stand?

-"Stay Confident to be Empowered". Oh Yeh? Easier said than done!

Such painful questions churn in the mind. Do they trouble others too?

I quite drifted away when she was saying.......

You are not alone. Most people have thoughts of self-doubt. In moments of decision, you have a conversation in your mind with your limiting beliefs. Such thoughts chain you down. Prevent you from doing what comes naturally to you.

When Circus Elephants are babies, their leg is chained to a strong peg. They fidget and tug to get free, and are unable to do so. As they grow, they are strong enough to uproot trees. However, they have decided in their mind that they can't get their leg free and have stopped trying since years. So even as fully grown elephants, they are still chained the same way, and they remain there.

This chain on the elephant's leg is similar to the chain we tie up our mind with. Thoughts of self-doubt. Limiting beliefs that never let us move forward.

Such negative thoughts make you feel bad and sad.

You have fears within, such as:

-What will people say?

-How can I answer back to my husband or mother-in-law or elders or boss?

-Will they think I am rude, if I answer?

-What if I lose my job?

-What do I do? What do I say? How do I say it?

-Whatever I say, they will run me down.

And the list continues…….

Do you feel stuck in life with these disturbing thoughts that pull you down? Well, whatever you think is what manifests in life. If you think you can do it, you will. If you think you can't, that's true too.

Life is given to us by God with love and care. We always have reasons to celebrate, nature renewing itself every day, our friends around us, the job that provides our livelihood, the miracles we see every day.

However, we insist on focusing only on the dark spots, the health issues that bother us, the lack of money, the complicated relationship with a family member, the disappointment with a friend, etc. The dark spots are very small compared to everything we have in our lives, but they are the ones that pollute our minds. Take your eyes away from the black spots in your life.

Life is a bag of good and bad things. We all have positives and negatives along the way. But we must always concentrate greater on the positives for a healthy and happy life. Life goes on no matter what. So, do not waste your time thinking about the negatives. They steal your self confidence and self-esteem. Enjoy each one of your blessings, each moment that life gives you. Be happy and live a life positively!

Everything happens twice in your life. Once in your mind and once in reality.

So, what you focus on, will happen in your life. If you focus on your negative thoughts and these take up your energies through the day, all your fears will materialise in your life. Most people focus more on the dark side of life and let their fears grip them. However, if you are able to have positive thoughts in your mind and focus on them, your life will be 'As you like it'.

In life, things happen around us, things happen to us, but the only thing that truly matters is how you choose to respond to it and what you make out of it.

Life actually does not happen to you, but for you.

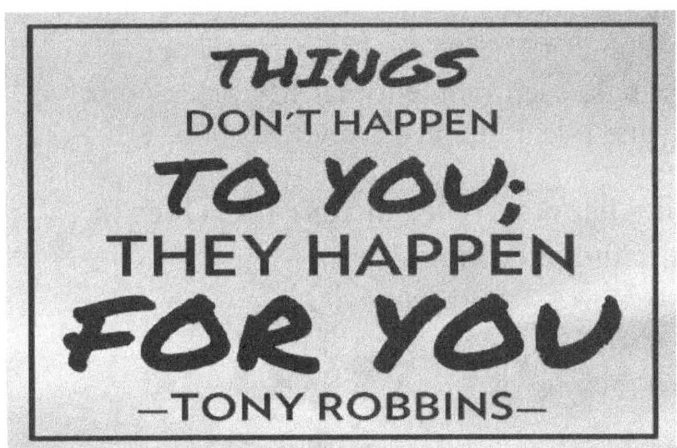

Life is all about learning, adapting and converting all the challenges that we experience into something positive.

Start taking tiny steps and very small actions to rebuild your confidence and empower yourself. Rome was not built in a day. So, this too will take time, however, take the first step which will in itself empower you to take the next. And the wheel will start to roll and gain momentum gathering powerful confidence in every area of your life.

Focus on creating magic out of adversities. Tell yourself, let the adversities come, they only help me to make myself stronger each time.

Our life is God's gift to us. What we do with it, is our gift to God.

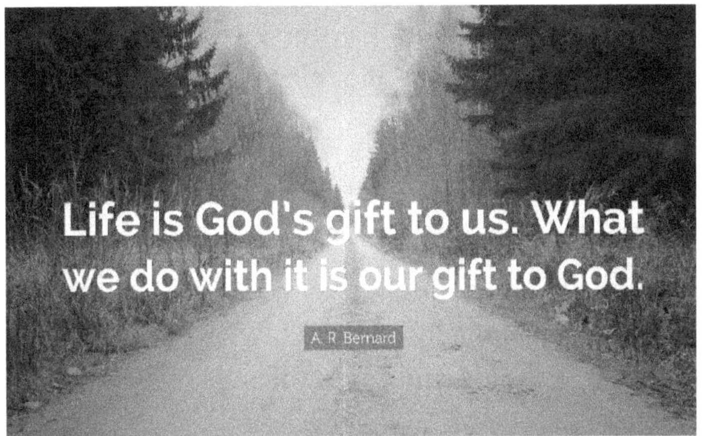

Confidence comes from within. Everyone has it. You need to tap the source in yourself. Start in small beginnings, one step at a time. Slowly but surely you are on your journey to empower yourself.

Like the Nike slogan, "Just Do It!"

What gives you the strength to have positive thoughts in your mind? It's your beliefs.

Belief in yourself and belief in your Creator.

Positive thoughts with belief in yourself give you confidence to take action and clarity of what exactly you want.

When I was a little girl, elders used to ask – What do you want to be when you grow up?

My answer was, 'I would like to be a Lady at Large, with a big bungalow, with flowers in the front, fruits on the side and vegetables grown in the backyard'.

Everyone would tell me what is this long story and laugh at my dream. My aunt used to tell me, so you want to be nothing of significance. Mention a profession like most children. What is this! My father used to joke that he would have to go out with a lantern to search for a husband who has all of that. I just knew what I wanted and did not budge.

Well, my father did not have to do anything like that. The man of my dreams came to me not on a horse back, but on a BSA Gold Star Motorcycle.

He had a beautiful bungalow just as I had dreamt about.

Everyone in the family was surprised. My grandma was no more. However, my grandpa was very proud of me and loved him at first sight. He said this man has a wonderful aura and will make you extremely happy in life.

Whenever I believe in something with my heart and soul, I am able to achieve it and this gets my confidence levels up. Being confident, I become capable of manifesting the results I desire.

However, not getting attached to the result, is the secret.

I was very close to my grandparents. I was very blessed to have them in my life. They were such

evolved souls and practiced the power of positive thinking in their lives. They have taught me many of life's lessons and inculcated great values in me. Today, my strength, my confidence comes from all of that.

Belief and confidence in myself helped me to take action and move forward in life. This result becomes my reference point. I have overcome challenges before, and I can do it once more. This feeling empowers me to face the challenge head on, with the right spirit, right mindset, clarity and confidence. Lights the fire within me, and with faith by my side, I feel totally empowered.

We are capable of so much more than we realize of our own confidence and courage. We can just release our control of structures that hold us to the ground, and see how far we can fly with our own power.

Throughout the forest of our lives there are many so-called branches and trees on which we rely on. And while sometimes we do need recovery and shelter, we can also learn as we grow, that these sources of safety do not always last – what is really lasting and permanent rests within us, in the form of positive self-esteem and belief in our own unique abilities.

The power of your own mind is the most amazing asset you have.

There was a business executive who was deep in debt and could see no way out. Creditors were closing in on him. Suppliers were demanding payment. He sat on the park bench, head in hands, wondering if anything could save his company from bankruptcy.

Suddenly an old man appeared before him. "I can see that something is troubling you," he said. After listening to the executive's woes, the old man said, "I believe I can help you." He asked the man his name, wrote out a cheque, and pushed it into his hand saying, "Take this money. Meet me here exactly one year from today, and you can pay me back at that time." Then he turned and disappeared as quickly as he had come.

The business executive saw in his hand a cheque for $500,000, signed by John D. Rockefeller, then one of the richest men in the world! "I can erase my money worries in an instant!" he realized. But instead, the executive decided to put the uncashed cheque in his safe. Just knowing it was there might give him the strength to work out a way to save his business, he thought.

With renewed optimism, he negotiated better deals and extended terms of payment. He closed several big sales. Within a few months, he was out of debt and making money once again. Exactly one year later, he returned to the park with the uncashed cheque. At the agreed-upon time, the old man appeared. But just as the executive was about to hand back the cheque and share his success story, a nurse came running up and grabbed the old man. "I'm so glad I caught him!" she cried. "I hope he hasn't been bothering you. He's always escaping from the rest home and telling people he's John D. Rockefeller." And she led the old man away by the arm.

The astonished executive just stood there, stunned. All year long he'd been wheeling and dealing, buying and selling, convinced he had half a million dollars behind him. Suddenly, he realized that it wasn't the money, real or imagined, that had turned his life around. It was his newfound self-confidence that gave him the power to achieve anything he went after.

So, you see, only you can change your life. Just believe in yourself. Boost your self-confidence. Empower yourself and see the magic happen in your life.

Self-Confidence is a Super-Power. Once you start to believe in yourself, magic starts happening.

That is what I will tell you in my upcoming book.

Till then,

Stay Confident Be Empowered.

CHAPTER 2

Vinay Kumar

Vinay Kumar is a Peak Performance Coach and now Author.

He has worked as a Software Engineer.

He was a shy, underconfident young man who is now a confident man on a mission to help people discover their own true potential and live a joyful life.

He is a lifetime volunteer for social activities.

BEING CURIOUS & BEING FOCUSED

Being Curious:

Curious: It's a Super Power and hunger to know Everything.

Curiosity is an innate, natural, and universal capacity that we all have, and knowing how it works from a neurobiological perspective is the first step to reawakening our childlike fascination and tapping into its potential.

"I have no special talents. I am only passionately curious". - **Albert Einstein**

Curiosity Induces two flavours- **Interest** and **Deprivation**.

Interest - pleasurable feeling when you have the hunger to know something which interests you. Pleasant state.

Eg: When you want to explore something new which is unexplored, learning something new, simply gives a feeling of excitement.

Deprivation - is when you don't know about something which you want to know. It's a state of mind until you know whic you don't know about. This can cause the stress of not knowing.

Eg: When you are in a meeting, you got a message on phone. Your desire to know the message.

Why do we have curiosity in the first place?
Curiosity builds on the evolutionarily conserved, reward-based learning mechanisms in our brains.

Reward-based learning relies on positive and negative reinforcement. You want to do more of the things that feel good and less of things that feel bad. Back in caveman days, this was important for helping us to find food (feeling good) and avoid danger (feeling bad). It is a trait of a human being that is evolved for having awareness of the surroundings and various subjects he or she is involved in.

In present times, I believe we lead better lives, run better businesses, and have more fulfilling work experiences when we are more curious. Being curious is a licence to explore and experiment. It allows you to try your hand at new things and follow opportunities that you might ordinarily be closed to.

How to be Curious…?

I am going to ask you a question and I want you to think deeply about it for the next few minutes.

And then I want you to write down every answer that comes into your mind. Here we go:

"Why do you want to be more Curious?"

You want to know more.

So that you can use the knowledge in your various spheres of life.

That's why you need to **keep asking "why"** to keep going into deeper levels of why, you need to be more Curious.

I'm going to do the exercise on myself:

1. ***Why*** *do you want to be more curious?*

Since I want to know more about my interests.

2. ***Why?***

Since I want to use the knowledge, I have acquired.

3. ***Why?***

Since it gets clarity on various subjects of my knowledge.

4. ***Why?***

Since I feel the Universe will open up to me to fulfil my quest for curiosity.

5. ***Why?***

Learning becomes effortless when you are curious.

What are some of the ways to be Curious in Life?

Before knowing ways to be curious, make a list of activities that makes you curious.

That's wonderful.

I believe you have written few things which make you curious.

Some of the Ways to be curious:

1. Read different subjects and follow your interests.
2. Read physical books.
3. Be willing to ask dumb questions. Ask "What if?"
4. Think curiously before searching Google to find answers.
5. Experiment on different things.
6. Follow your passions wherever they take you.
7. Get out of the office at lunchtime, so that you can explore new places to eat.
8. Be an ideas collector.
9. Allow your mind to wander.
10. Feed your passions.
11. Reach out to people you admire.
12. Talk to a stranger. Listen to people. Just out of curiosity.
13. Explore the unfamiliar.

14. Observe your surroundings.
15. Carry a camera with you.
16. Explore the areas where ever you go for business trips.
17. Walk around a city without a map.
18. Read news from multiple sources to get different perspectives.
19. Extend your network.
20. Think like a kid. Be silly to know the Universe.

Blocking curiosity:

- Overconfidence—we may think we know more than we do.
- Being so self-absorbed that we are unaware of our surroundings.
- Negative Emotions such as guilt, fear, anxiety, and external pressures such as threats and punishment, all can diminish our curiosity.

Being Focused:

Focus: To give attention, effort, to one particular subject, situation, or person rather than another.

If there's one thing, we could all probably use a lot is the ability to focus. But telling yourself to stay focused on a task, especially a mundane one, is often a lot easier said than done.

Staying focused can help you accomplish a variety of professional and personal tasks. It gives results by accomplishing the important tasks first.

For Example,

1. **Barak Obama**: when writing the book "A Promised Land", he mostly wrote in the nights after his family slept, because of deep focus.
2. **Bill Gates**: Plans "Think Weeks" two times per year, where he secludes in a private space where he removes all the distractions and focuses on deep thoughts, ideas, projects.

How to be focused...?

1. **Vision and mission** - clarity upon vision and mission is very important to be focused on. Make a vision statement for 1month, 1quarter, half-year, annual, 3years, 5years, etc.

2.**Work Space** - Keep your workspace organized. Select a space where there are no disturbances and distractions to work on your craft. Like private rooms, library. If possible, seclude yourself or plug in your earbuds to make the environment silent for yourself, etc. Few may like to be silent and few may like to have soft music in the background.

3. **Prioritize the tasks** for the day in terms of 4 quadrants - Urgent, Not Urgent, Important, and Not important. Complete the Deep Work first than the Shallow Work.

4. **Pomodoro Technique** - to work on your craft, work for 50 minutes and take a break for 10 min and get back to work. So that the focus is realigned.

5. **Time Blocks** - work in Time blocks, blocking the time and dates as per your important tasks and priorities. Put down on paper, listing the hours on left side, and on right side write the activities planned to finish the tasks in the stipulated time.

6. **Re-energize time** - Have time for rest so that your mind re-energizes for more focused work.

7. **Routine** - have a routine so that you are disciplined to focus on your tasks.

8. **Purpose** - your purpose should be strong. Your "Why" should be very strong to be focused on the task.

9. To stay focused throughout the day and remain productive, it's important to build healthy habits like getting enough sleep and exercising regularly.

10. **Multitasking** and social media can cause distractions during work, so it's best to limit them.

11. Make a **to-do list**.

12. Give yourself a **time limit** for each task.

13. Avoid **online distractions**- keep your electronic devices away. Keep your mobile on Detox mode (Use Detox App).

14. **Avoid physical distractions**- avoid talking to people when deeply focused.

15. **Multi-task** less to enhance your focus.

16. Improve your focus stamina. **Daily practice** makes you focused.

17. Take a few **Deep Breaths** to settle your mind and help you focus.

18. **Get used to boredom**, so that you can get back to focused work quickly. Don't get involved in distractions in this period that will carry you away.

19. Whenever you feel distracted practice **Mindfulness**, deep breathing, a small walk, stretching your body, looking at the distant objects, etc.

20. **Minimize multitasking**. Be focused on one task at a time.

How do you improve focus and concentration?

Sit or work in environments where it's peaceful and serene where there are no distractions and disturbances. Some people need total silence spaces and some need soft soothing music in the background.

You're more likely to stay focused when you're working on something you're good at and enjoy doing.

If you can delegate some work to others then it would give you time to work on the most critical tasks of yours.

Stare at something like Fire, Ants, Insects. Observe them, their activities continuously for few minutes every day. It increases the focusing capabilities.

Food For being Focused -Concentrated and Being Intense:

Have more raw food in your diet like salads, fruits, sprouts, etc. which are light and need less energy to digest.

Foods that take more time to digest would make you feel lethargic or drowsy, than the natural foods which are easily digested like Salads, fruits, Sprouts, etc. This keeps you super awake, supercharged and active. Also keeps you focused on the tasks.

Hydrate your body well. Drink at least 8 glasses of water per day.

Exercises to the body keeps you active and healthy. Stretching of the body muscles on regular intervals keeps you active.

Being Curious, Focused and Intense takes regular practice on day-to-day basis to intensify the superpowers.

By being Consistent, Practice regularly, Perseverant, and Patient, you can Achieve your dreams.

CHAPTER 3

Niranjan Deshpande

Niranjan Deshpande is a Storyteller and a Growth Hacker Coach for Mindset.
He has worked with AV Birla, Wizcraft and Leo Burnett.
Actor by Heart and Marketer by Profession.
Coach Niranjan loves to network with people to listen to their stories and experiences.
His mission is to enlighten people's lives by helping them to achieve what they like and/or aspire to achieve.

TO BE OR NOT TO BE

"Yes, I am stuck now," Anthony said.
"To be or not to be...that is the question!!" He was trying to mimic 'Helmet', the famous Shakespearean character.

Anthony, a colleague and friend of mine was telling me about his current situation. MBA from a top B-School in the country and with a remarkable journey of career in marketing industry. Married to a super woman and father of two kids and one dog (as what he always keeps claiming).

Three months back he had decided to leave his top most position in our company and he had sent his resignation letter to our HR department. As he was serving notice period he used to come to office on a daily basis.

Our friendship was more than a decade old, and so was our professional relationship. We often kept consulting each other for our decisions and we usually conducted our consultation sessions either in his cabin or my cabin and of course over a snack-bite or a cup of coffee.

I was aware that Anthony had decided to quit his job as he was looking forward to starting a new business on his own. Last one and half years he was working after office hours, towards achieving his goal. For him it was a side hustle. He was busy learning new things, building networks, working out budgets and so on. And suddenly today, after this long weekend, he came to me saying he shouldn't have resigned as he is still in a dilemma whether to start his business or not.

It was completely shocking for me and Anthony's dilemma was clearly visible on his face. After spending a few more minutes with him, feeling his dilemma, I told him to wait until evening, so that we could discuss why he was in this situation.

I called my wife and explained Anthony's situation and told her that I might join her late for the dinner. After leaving office, Anthony and I went to our favourite coffee shop.

I listened to Anthony patiently. I gave a thought to all the points he had spoken about, and decided to help him to come out of his dilemma.

I asked him a few questions about his decision to resign three months back, and what happened over this long weekend that he started doubting his own abilities forcing him to revoke his resignation.

In his explanations to my questions, Anthony told me that when he resigned, he had two choices - Option one - to follow his dream and start a new business on his own or Option two - to join another organisation in the same industry.

He was very aware about the consequences of his decision, like not getting enough business in the beginning, compromise on personal life, facing competition in the market and so on. He had also explained this to his wife and his kids. They were very supportive and that's why he was clearly steering towards his goal.

Being a dynamic person, Anthony was popular amongst his colleagues. He was a person who was very ambitious and optimistic. He always worked very efficiently and his excellence and efficiency made him a catalyst.

He was quite sure about setting up his new business and he had achieved enough skills to thrive into it. As he had strong connections in his network, he was always getting enough help whenever he needed so.

Anthony kept sharing his answers and I kept wondering more and more, what might be the reason which made Anthony to doubt his own decision of starting a new business.

Five years back, he had dreamt about starting a new business. He designed his complete roadmap spending more than three years after that. For last two years, he was building his network around it. He learned and acquired new skills for the same in the last one year. He had built everything around his biggest dream, step-by-step as per his roadmap and suddenly he was backing off?

Few moments passed by thinking about it and then I asked Anthony when he decided to revoke his resignation. He told me that just over the last long weekend he had given it a thought and then he decided to continue doing the job and dropped the idea of starting his business.

What made him take that decision? I was still wondering in my mind. Even last week when we met Anthony was in a very good mood and was enthusiastically sharing the details about receiving his registration certificate for his business. In fact, he was going to a getaway resort along with his family and friends to celebrate it.

It clicked to me then, that's when Anthony must have changed his mind.

So, I asked Anthony, "How did your trip go?"

He said "Went very well! We all enjoyed it a lot. We were 3 families and we had a blast!!"

"And what was your friends' reactions about your upcoming business plans?
I hope they must have shared their suggestions also!!" I asked curiously.

"Yeah, they all were happy and praised my plans too! But Vikram and Rajesh…" And Anthony's mobile buzzed, displaying one of his clients' names. Anthony answered the call and started speaking with his client.

I remembered Anthony telling me about Vikram and Rajesh some months back, they were Anthony's school friends. Though three of them had lost touch, they recently met at last year's school reunion, and then they started meeting again. The recent trip was long due on their schedule.

After Anthony finished the call, I again asked him about Rajesh's and Vikram's reactions. Anthony was totally in distress. He told me how both of them pointed out loopholes in his business plans. They gave him examples of failed businesses too. Anthony felt helpless when both of them, after a few rounds of drinks, started convincing their points to Rosy-Anthony's wife, in front of all the families.

That night, Anthony could not sleep well. Next day, on their way back home, he was driving quietly. In the evening when Rosy had a chance to have a few moments alone with Anthony, she asked him why he was so upset. Though Anthony denied at the time, he was upset as he was actually thinking about the earlier day's discussions and incidents. His mindset was changing.

And with the same mindset he spoke with me that morning in the office.
My mind was racing. I went to the coffee shop counter and ordered some snacks and two more coffees for us.

I told Anthony to be at ease and have his favourite coffee along with the snacks.

I asked him some questions about Rajesh and Vikram. Did Anthony achieve happiness by spending his time with them on their trip? Could he really celebrate his success with them or was it just an illusion in his mind? Whether he or his wife really liked their company?

Anthony replied to all my questions with a big 'NO'!!!

I shared my concerns with Anthony. I told him why he should be choosy about the people with whom he spends his time. They should inspire him with their honest opinions and positive attitude. They should bring some value to his life. And if they are not doing so, he should just kick them out of his life!!

I told Anthony what my mentor Arfeen Khan says, "Having great people around you can greatly help you not only to stay committed to your quest but also allows you to enjoy the ride. For thoughts to keep you going, you will need a dose of unconditional love, cheering on, being appreciated by the people around you!!"

I gave him an example of a bee. How a bee collects honey and preserves it for the future in the same way you choose people and save them for your future.

Anthony's eyes started sparkling as he was carefully listening to me. He got up and gave me a tight hug before we called it a night.

Next day, when I walked in my Cabin, a small bottle of honey with a greeting card was placed on my table saying, "Thank you for enlightening my mind. From now on, no more 'To Be or Not To Be'!" With Love -Anthony.

CHAPTER 4

Nagesh Babu Maile

The author of this chapter is Bangalore's First Confidence & Mental Toughness Coach and he is currently working as a software professional in the VLSI Industry. He did his Master's and Bachelor's Engineering degree from Jawaharlal Nehru Technological University, Hyderabad. He had experience in Industrial Instrumentation and Automation. With his passion to Teach, he taught under-graduate and post-graduate students in various Engineering colleges and university.

He is born and brought up from Andhra Pradesh and currently settled in Bangalore.

He is on a mission "to help 100,000 working professionals in building confidence and mental toughness".

SECRETS OF MENTAL STRENGTH

Mental strength is the ability of a person to consciously and acutely control their feelings and emotions, thoughts and decisions. It is the ability of a person to sustain under constant stress, strain, and pressure. It is the ability of a person to face the challenges courageously and keep themselves ready for any challenge in their life. It is mandatory for every individual to build mental strength in order to live their life in a better way.

Mental strength is not an option, it is mandatory.

Most of the people especially the software professionals don't come across any problems. Most of them are lucky enough to get campus placement and some might get placement off the campus. Such people who are living without any worries right from their childhood, may never know how strong they are mentally so long as their life goes on smoothly. They experience their real mental strength when they come across problems.

1. Discover our core baselines:

You have developed your core baselines about yourselves, your lives and the world you are living in. These core baselines actually determine the way you are seeing the world.

Your core baselines are those which are developed without you realizing over the years and they largely depend upon your past experiences.

Whether you are aware of them or not, these core baselines influence mental strength in terms of your thoughts and decisions. These baselines will influence your behaviour and also decides how you react to the emotions. Whatever the decisions you may take, they are interlinked with your core baselines.

They will determine whether you are happy with the decisions you made or not. Some decisions may make you happy and some may not, it is all dependant on whether they satisfy your core baselines or not.

For example, one of my core baselines is togetherness. I can do wonders when I work together with others, whereas I feel stuck when I do it alone.

This book is the best example of togetherness as my core baseline. The thought of writing a book is not new, it was my old plan. Whatever the reason, I could not complete my book from the past 10 years. Finally, I'm writing this co-authored book together with my friends.

You should discover your core baselines so that you can progress in life with fulfilment and happiness. Whenever they are met, you will feel happy because your decision is fulfilling them.

When they fail to meet you will feel unhappy, because your decisions are not fulfilling your baselines.

So, core baselines play an important role in building mental strength and hence one has to discover them, which is the first step towards building the mental strength.

2. Discover how you are hardwired:

Hope you are aware of the Law of Attraction. Whatever thoughts come in our mind it is going to happen in reality.

Everything happens twice in your life.

First in your mind and second in reality.

Let me share my life example. One day we travelled from Vijayawada to Bangalore by train on a 3day vacation. My spouse saw in her dream that she lost all the gold and hence she took the gold and carried in her handbag. We reached Bangalore and spent 3 days at my father-in-law's residence happily. We caught the train in Sheshadripuram railway station, Bangalore for our return journey. My elder son was 1 year old and stepped down from the train following his grandmother. In a hurry to catch the kid, my wife left her handbag on the seat and ran to bring the child back. In the meantime, someone stole the hand-bag which had all the gold my spouse dreamt about before we started this tour and it was not traced even after complaining to the Railway police. So, whatever we think in our mind, is going to happen in reality.

Complaint lodged in railway station for the Theft of handbag

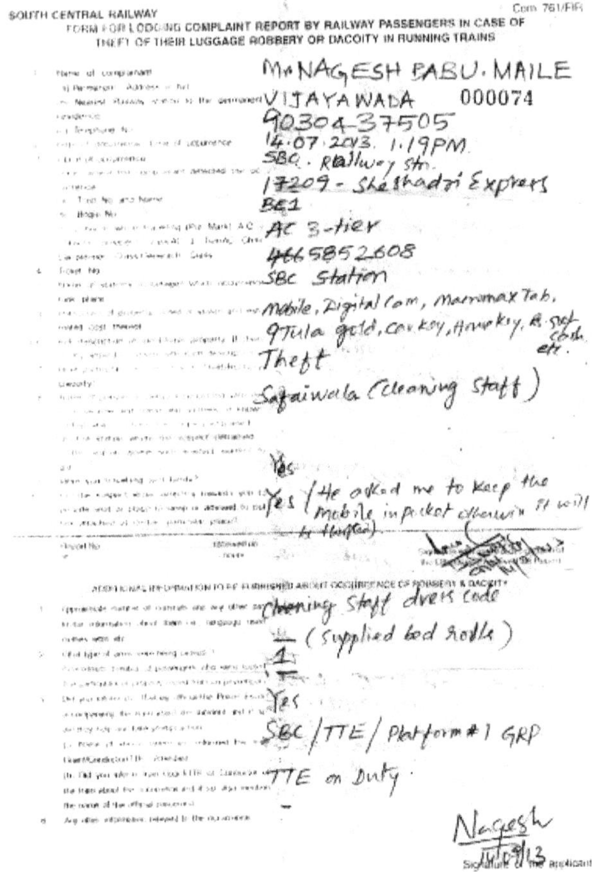

If you think negatively, you are going to attract the negativity. If you think positively, you are going to attract the positivity. Negative thinking drains out your mental energy whereas positive thinking boosts your mental energy.

For example, if you are participating in a race, and if you believe that you'll never succeed in winning the race, there is no probability for you winning the race, because you will start the race with the lowest state of your mind and your mental energy is very low. The consequences are that you will lose the race.

If you believe that you will win the race, there is a probability that you may win the race because you will start the race with your highest state of mind and your mental energy is very high. The chances of you winning the race are more when you put your 100% effort to win the race. That means you are focusing on what is in your control.

Jamaican sprinter Usain Bolt won

three gold medals at the 2008 Olympic Games in Beijing, China, and he became the first man in Olympic history to win both the 100meter, and 200meter races in record times. This was possible for him because he participated in the race with positive thoughts to win the race with his highest state of mind. His mental energy was very high at that time. Also, he gave his 100% effort. All that made him win the race.

The more you think negatively, the lesser energy you will have to do what you want to do. Every negative thought will drain your mental energy. So, save your mental energy with your positive thinking and put your effort 100% so that you can achieve whatever you want to achieve.

It is hence very important to develop a habit of discovering how you are hardwired by means of your negative thoughts so that you can consciously control your thoughts and reduce the dissipation of your mental strength.

3. Reframe your negative coding:

Whatever the negative thoughts you have in your mind, try to spend some time to think about them and understand that they are holding you back. Over a period of time, these thoughts become your codes.

Codes such as "Everyone is always against me", "No one loves me" will always de-energize you mentally and they can hold you back from moving ahead. Such negative codes will not allow you to reach your full potential.

Moreover, your mind will start hunting for the evidences to prove that the code that is formed in your mind is true.

Let us consider one incident from my real life. I tend to have negative thoughts that, "No one loves me and no one cares for me among my family and friends". Now, my brain starts looking for the evidences.

One day, when I went to school along with my grandfather, to take my transfer certificate, my grandfather told me, looking at the certificate, "He is not your father but he is your maternal uncle. Your mother passed away when you were 7 days old and your father abandoned you after that incident. Your maternal uncle graciously took over your responsibility as if you were his own son".

My brain immediately caught that point and in no time, my inner voice told me "Oh Nagesh, you are an orphan. That's why no one loves you and no one cares about you among your family and friends".

This is how our thoughts are integrated as codes and that is how we give meaning to the world we live in, in reality.

So, collect your negative thoughts before they get converted into codes. Even you can collect all the negative codes you have and reframe each and every negative thought to a positive thought, because all the positive thoughts are productive in nature.

"Everybody loves me and everybody cares for me in my family and friends". This positive code gave me energy and helped me to reach my highest potential. This was how I reframed all my negative thoughts to positive thoughts and now I'm the best version of myself.

4. Show your gratitude:

Having gratitude or thankfulness to what you have today, is a key to building mental strength. Showing gratitude consistently helps you to reduce your stress and it gives you peace of mind and keeps you mentally strong.

I practice gratitude early in the morning as soon as I wake-up from the bed, daily. It has become a habit to me. I plan my day with gratitude and it keeps me motivated and gives energy throughout the day.

I am thankful to my foster parents who brought me up and also to my parents who gave me birth. I'm thankful to my brothers and sisters. I'm thankful to my spouse and kids. I am thankful to my family members, relatives and friends. I am thankful to my colleagues and managers. I'm thankful to my coaches and mentors. I am thankful to everything I have in my life and every single person I am connected with.

5. Increase your Endurance:

Life is like a roller coaster. There will be ups and downs in the journey called Life. Every individual experiences, emotions, stress, strain, pressure and challenges in his or her life. There are no excuses in lives of mentally strong persons.

You should increase your endurance and ability to sustain constant stress, strain and pressure. You should face whatever challenges come your way, so that you get mentally strong.

We give great honour to those who endure under suffering.

Being mentally strong, you need to be acutely aware of your emotions so that you can you can control your emotions instead of you being controlled by them. You can control your emotions by practice. You may feel difficulty at the beginning, but you can get better at it as your confidence levels increase.

Mentally strong people will accept each challenge as an opportunity to experience and they will never treat it as a problem, instead they build confidence by facing them.

I always stepped out of my comfort zone and looked for new challenges. I lived most of my life under constant stress, strain and pressure. Even now, I'm writing this book today 20th April 2021 at 2.40 am which tells that I am working out of my comfort zone.

There will be no wine if grapes are not pressed, there is no perfume if the flowers are not crushed, so don't be afraid if there is pressure in your life. It will bring best out of you.

6. Mentally prepare yourself:

Catastrophic impact of COVID is that the entire world got affected due to coronavirus and the whole world is experiencing uncertainty in all aspects and the outcomes are fatal.

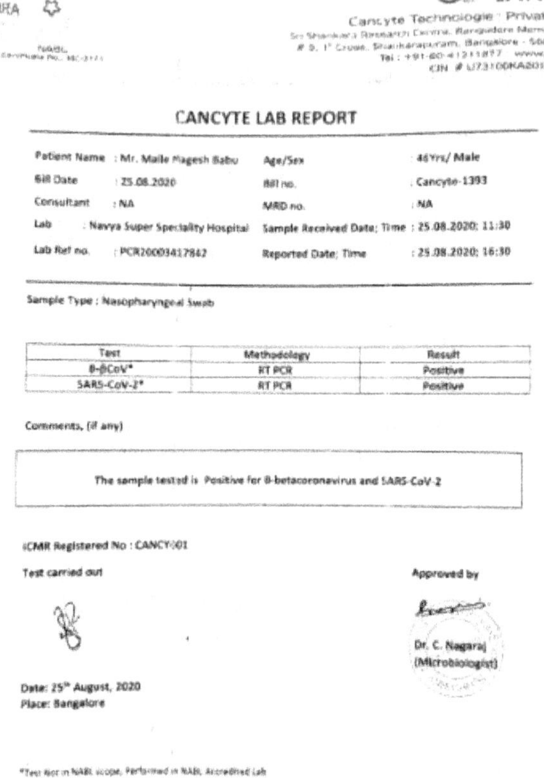

Because of the corona virus pandemic most of the people are experiencing constant stress because of the fear of getting affected with the virus. Poor and Mediocre people are worried about how to pay the bills.

Mentally strong people will not lose confidence, instead they will be mentally prepared to experience the tough time.

Last year, I was tested positive for COVID and I was in home quarantine for 15 days. Even after 15 days, my health was not stabilized, so I was admitted in hospital for 10 days which cost me more than 4 lakhs. I got medical insurance for 2 lakhs and the rest I paid from my pocket. Being myself mentally strong, I could manage to control my emotions, stress and everything.

7. Track your strength:

Most people will look for physical strength but ignore the mental strength. Having mental strength and doing mental exercises as mentioned above are equally important as physical health.

One cannot say I am mentally strong and stop exercising as mentioned above. Like our physical workouts, we should also plan for the mental workouts.

Today, people are busy and mostly mediocre. They are lazy to do physical workouts, quoting lack of time and some have a very easy excuse of the pandemic. Whatever the reason may be, it is a good habit to do physical exercise daily because you can be mentally strong when you are physically fit.

You should plan your day so that you spend at least some minimum time for your gratitude, physical workout and mental workout.

Keep your eye on your progress towards achieving mental strength. It is not that you got the mental strength today means you will be having that mental strength forever. You should keep on increasing your mental strength, as this is just a beginning.

Consciously control your thoughts, feelings and emotions so that it helps you to develop your self-confidence. Also keep track of "What you want to improve, where you stand today, and how much you want to accomplish tomorrow".

Remember one thing: "There is always a room for improvement" in every aspect of your life. When you track your day-to-day progress in building the mental strength, it can help to enhance your ability.

It is not the physical strength that makes you feel strong; it is the mental strength that makes you feel strong.

CHAPTER 5

Sonia Aggarwal

Sonia Aggarwal was born in New Delhi, India, which is a beautiful city of Heritage. Since childhood she has a passion for creative arts. She has a keen interest in sketching, dancing and she is inclined toward literature reading.

She is a Training & Human Resource Professional since 2008. She is a Graduate from Delhi University & holds a Master's degree in HR.

She is a mother and has very high family values. Her relations are her power and inspiration. While gaining her experience in people management, she also developed a passion for writing down her ideas & thoughts. This is her first published work & she is a blooming Author.

Her mission is to coach people in fields of relationship and self-awareness.

THE OTHER HALF OF YOUR LIFE – WORK-LIFE BALANCE

Most of the people tend to get stretched between their professional and Personal Lives. Of course, both are equally important. One has a flavor of Achievement and the other has of Enjoyment. But at any given point in time, if the proportion of any of the flavors' goes wrong, the taste of life becomes bad.

Most of us are aware of this concept; no matter we are professionally engaged or not. Besides our personal lives, our work lives are undoubtedly the space in which we've seen the biggest changes. Apart from the obvious increase of working from home, one common sentiment we've heard from so many people is that now that they are working remotely, they are struggling to balance their work lives with their personal lives.

With the increasing amount of technology, Work-life balance has become a topical issue that eliminates the importance of physical presence in defining the work-life balance. In the previous era, it was difficult or impossible to take work home and so there was a clear line between professional and personal life.

The increase in cloud-based software and the proliferation of the internet has made it much easier for employees to be at work 24*7, erasing the defining line between professional and personal. It has become a big challenge to make time for family, friends, community participation, spirituality, personal growth, self-care, and other personal activities, in addition to the demands of the workplace.

Majority of the working professional; whether working as an employee or on their own; fails to create a work-life balance. They fail to learn the importance of both the flavors; Achievement & Enjoyment. In most cases, it is the work that has been prioritized, and what suffers is the personal aspects of life including Health, Relationships with friends & family, self-improvement and Fun time. And the reason is that work provides financial support which is commonly considered as Achievement and the most important factor for a happy life. But is that true?

How does it feel when your child sits with you and shares his happy moments? Have you given it a thought that how does it feels when you have a share of your presence in those talks? What is important? You child sharing smiles with you or sharing the story of smiles with you? Have you ever thought that how important is it to spend some time with friends and have fun-time? There is a famous saying that "Laughter is the best medicine". Science has proven that Laughter improves the function of blood vessels and increases blood flow giving a healthy heart. It boosts your immune system. A good, hearty laugh relieves physical tension and stress. Laughter triggers the release of endorphins, the body's natural feel-good chemicals. Fun Time or Laughter does not only mean "Ha-Ha" happiness. It means Pride, Satisfaction, Happiness, Celebration, Love, A Sense of Well Being …all the Joys of Living.

Work-Life Balance does not only mean an equal balance. Trying to schedule an equal number of hours for each is usually unrewarding and unrealistic. The quality of hours is the most important factor. The best individual work-life balance will vary over time, often daily. The right balance for you today will probably be different for you tomorrow. The right balance for you when you are single will be different when you marry, or if you have children; when you start a new career versus when you are nearing retirement. The concept of one-size-fits-all doesn't imply here. The best work-life balance is different for each of us because we all have different priorities and different lives.

However, at the core of an effective work-life balance, we may see the importance of including both, Achievement and Enjoyment, in our daily lives. When you are considering your work-life balance, planning begins before you look for a job and accept a new position. First, take the time to determine your real-life needs from the broadest perspective. For example, you may be surprised to discover that how a lower-paying job with proximity to time spent with your children is preferable to another highly-paying option that takes you over an hour on the way.

Take control of your work schedule. Creating this balance is not a difficult task at all. There are many ways for it. Check out the below steps to improve work-life balance. There are defined ways to how an individual can maintain a proper work-life balance, some of which are:

1. Creating a plan at the workplace including leisure: Where an individual has to schedule his tasks, and divide time appropriately so that he has allocated appropriate time to his work and his career development goals and at the same time allotted time for leisure and personal development. Employees also use a compressed workweek plan to build a balance.

2. Exclude activities that waste energy and time: Individual should thoughtfully and judiciously avoid wasteful activities which demand a lot of time and energy and which in return do not produce output for either the work-life or the leisure life. If a person can do Effective time

management, it can help an employee be less stressed.

3. Delegating or Outsourcing work: It is important to ask for help, and if you can find others who want to learn, then it helps them also. People who are new managers, may not ask for help, as they might want to show that they can achieve success by themselves or seek the right answer for the solution, but that this might not be a good way. We all need to learn to be comfortable to ask for help.

4. Set enough time for relaxation: Relaxation provides better work-life balance and tends to improve productivity on the professional or the work front along with providing ample scope to develop the life part of the balance.

5. Prioritizing work: Often we do not give priority to work and end up doing a lot of work at the last minute. Better planning can help us save unnecessary time delays, which can be utilized by us for personal work.

Whether you're feeling the strain in your overall mental health, or you are struggling to create boundaries between work and life, it's time to make room for the changes and practices that can help you find balance.

There are several advantages of work-life balance. Some of them are discussed below:

1. Work-life balance increases motivation and helps us perform better at work & personal life.

2. It helps us to relieve our stress as we can spend leisure time with our near and dear ones.

3. Companies can maximize productivity from an employee who is rejuvenated and refreshed as compared to an overworked employee.

4. Healthy lifestyles can be maintained by having a work-life balance. This includes a good diet, regular exercises, etc.

5. Employees who are highly motivated can help the business grow as they are more attached to their job and careers.

A 2019 study by software company Rescue Time looked at 185 million hours of working time. Here are some key findings:

- Workers average just 2 hours and 48 minutes of productive device time a day.
- 21% of working hours are spent on entertainment, news and social media.
- 28% of workers start their day before 8:30 a.m. (and 5% begin before 7 a.m.).
- 26% of work is done outside of regular working hours.
- We check email and instant messaging, on average, every 6 minutes.

- 40.1% of our day is spent multitasking with communication tools.

Following are a few more facts that are required to be kept under consideration while managing the balance between professional and personal spheres:

* Decide what is most sacred and precious to you, put a boundary around it, and talk to your manager about that boundary so it can be supported. Don't expect your manager to read your mind and know what you need most. These conversations need to be had in a deliberate manner. It may be your children, or it may be an ailing parent who you are caring for. It doesn't matter what it is.
* Take care of yourself. Although this is perhaps an overly used analogy you have to put the oxygen mask on yourself first on an airplane before you can help others. You have to be rested and healthy to truly be helpful to anyone. If you are good at your job and have a good boss, they will support you.
* Make sure you are seeing things clearly to make the wisest decision possible at the moment. I find meditation helps me have a perspective on tough decisions. But perhaps you need to take a walk, go for a run or sit on a decision for some time before you have the

answer. Anything that helps you see the problem from a broader view is helpful. As Shawn Anchor says in his talks and books about happiness, it doesn't matter if the glass is half empty or half full as long as you know there is a pitcher of water nearby.

* Don't attend meetings just for "face time." You know what these meetings look like. You know when you don't really need to be there. People are rarely promoted for face time. They are promoted for doing a good job and solving problems creatively. Don't give in to the pressure of attending a meeting that you are not going to make a meaningful contribution to, one that others can handle on their own. People know when you don't really need to be there. If anything, it can be detrimental to your career at times.

* Your time is your most precious commodity. You don't get to live forever and neither do the people you love. Remember this every day and be deliberate about how you spend your time.

* Stop worrying about what people think of your choices. It's your life, not theirs. You will never regret maintaining boundaries around what is sacred to you and you don't have to justify it to anyone. People aren't really thinking that much about you anyway. Get over yourself.

Defining work-life balance in the future can look like a worker and their employer sharing a belief that purpose at work and in life is paramount. There are several possible theories and policies that may begin affecting the future of work-life balance. The four-day workweek, for example, is catching on at many businesses and in many countries. Early findings indicate it may boost productivity, employee satisfaction, and work-life balance. There is also the question of work-life integration, which many experts believe work-life balance essentially leads to. These possibilities all hang over the future of work-life balance.

Defining and achieving the ideal work-life balance is something every individual employee will ultimately have to contend with themselves. Employers also need to understand the risks associated with burnout and not taking care of their employees' personal needs. The future of work-life balance will affect everyone, so everyone needs to give it necessary consideration.

CHAPTER 6

Kenneth Pinto

Kenneth started his journey in Hotels in 1981. He worked for around 20 years in the Hospitality Industry where he was the Regional Manager Training (S) with the Taj Group. In 2000 he started his own training organization running Business Etiquette and Customer Service focused workshops for corporate organizations & the Institute of Chartered Accountants of India.

He is a twice Certified Coach- IAC and Arfeen Khan. He says "For me, life was a roller coaster". Take charge of the Relationships in your life. Don't let anyone dictate the terms & run it. I wish I met a coach earlier who would have challenged me to find the answers, to walk through the difficult periods and take the right decisions.

When you live your life on your own terms the ride is awesome.

CREATING MAGICAL RELATIONSHIPS

You need to work on meaningful sustained relationships built on the pillars of traditions, customs, culture and the prevalent laws of the land to ensure mutual respect, fairness, trust, honesty & integrity in all aspects of our dealings with others.

Our Relationships in Life are determined by who we really are.

This is born out of our experiences and the people who surround us. Parents primarily in the early part, siblings, the extended family, religion, teachers, friends circle, the books and movies we see and now social media.

We are learning animals pick up survival instincts from our surroundings. Some adapt quickly and change their behaviour and make compromises while others stick to their core values and beliefs.

It is said that a man can be judged by the company he keeps. This takes me to the belief that one rotten apple can spoil the w

hole batch and there is plenty of evidence to this theory all around us. We see it happening in family, friends circle, and offices and in any situation where people are involved. The power of "ONE" cannot be undermined. It takes the first stone thrown to start a riot and then people mindlessly react without realizing what they are actually fighting for. A rumour started by a single irresponsible person can trigger chaos & in today's day and age with social media many of us have been victims of fake news.

Relationships are built layer upon layer over a period of time. There are different types of relationships we enter in our life span. Some are permanent and others fulfill a particular objective. Some people come into our lives for **A Reason; a Season or a Lifetime** describes the different relationships we have.
An important point for our reflection would be "what element of the relationship is critical to the

person" If this is not met, then the others pale in significance. Every element has its unique criticality and must compliment the other. This is essential to keep the bundle of elements intact.
Being on the same page is an expression we are familiar with in our dealings with others.

Broadly our relationships can be categorized into the following:
1. Intimate
2. Personal- family & friends
3. Official- colleagues
4. Business
5. Transactional

The foundation or first layer has many common elements:

E.g. Trust, integrity, respect, truthfulness, honesty, commitment, transparency, traditions, culture and laws.

The second layer will have different elements depending on the relationship.

E.g:
Intimate: Expressed love, Loyalty, empathy, hygiene, habits, care & concern.
Personal:
Family- Love, care& concern, kindness, being available, considerate, forgiving, tolerance, flexibility, empathy etc.
Friends-Care and concern, help, listen, borrow, lend etc.

Official: Teamwork, not gossiping, supportive, collaborative, cooperation, flexibility, timely feedback, appreciation etc.

Business: Brainstorm, accept, question, financial acumen etc.

Transactional: Time, quality, delivery etc.

Observing the above we see some commonalities that are important in most relationship.

So, what makes some relationships stronger than others?

This will require you to take it to the third level.

E.g: Intimate: Surprises, hugs, doing something your partner likes, holidays, gifts, appreciation etc.

Likewise, you can think of how to make each relationship you have stronger and lasting.

A bad relationship does not necessarily mean that all the elements are missing. It goes bad because one or more critical elements are not met which the other party values. Eg:

In an intimate relationship there is no trust.

In a family relationship there is no forgiveness.

In a friend's relationship you don't lend.

In an office relationship you are not much of a team player.

In a business relationship there is no integrity.

In a transactional relationship you don't deliver on time.

Why do relationships break?

Relationships as we now know are built on a variety of elements. When your relationships are nurtured and strong, built over time we tend to be forgiving and give the other the benefit. We also sometimes cling to the relationship because of social stigmas and economic and financial dependability.

But this too has a breaking point.

When a relationship is fragile it can snap easily.

The common factors that break up relationships can be attributed to the behavior we demonstrate: Attitude, arrogance, ego, ignorance, hidden agenda etc. which upset the other concerned party which ends the relationship.

There are four major outcomes in any relationship:

1. I win you lose
2. You win I lose
3. We both lose
4. We both win

I win you lose:

We have seen this happen many a time and at times we perpetrate this crime. It leaves one party feeling down and victimized. In the long run it will never survive unless the victim has no choice or chooses to be trampled upon. Surprisingly some people choose to be victimized and seem to enjoy playing the role of martyr.

You win I lose:

This is a double-edged sword. It can be used at times to trap a person and the turn the tables on them. It shows the carrot initially and then the stick. An example could be. Join me for this free experience and when you get hooked the charges start. One needs to be extremely careful when you are offered a free lunch. This too leaves one party feeling cheated. The other reason could be you genuinely want the other to benefit and you are blessed with a large heart with no expectation.

We both lose

This can be related to the quote 'cut your nose to spite your face'. The dog in the manger attitude some develop. The person usually has either had some traumatic experience which has left them bitter or is a sadist by nature. Sometimes the person feels if I have suffered this, others too should experience my pain.

We both win

Nothing can be more rewarding than this situation where both parties work in harmony so the result is not 1+1 but 1+1++.

This requires a genuine feeling of gratitude for opportunities and making the most of them for the mutual benefit of all involved. There is a different chemistry in this relationship. Is based on love, fulfilment and the firm belief that you put in your best effort to deliver the result that makes everyone happy.

While most of us usually work in one dimension at times people may alter depending on the situation. The best state to operate in is by far the win-win state.

When a person operates from the I win you lose state they end up being the most hated person.

When you operate from the I lose you lose state again you are hated.

When you operate from the I lose you win state it shows benevolence and a large heart or there may be a hidden agenda.

When you operate from the I win you win state all are happy.

How do we start operating in the win-win state?

It takes a strong will & commitment to apply this rule in all our dealings with others across the board and we cannot waiver. In the long run life will be a journey you enjoyed leaving a legacy. You will be remembered as a person who lived his life with integrity and honour.

Is this journey easy? Definitely not. It is extremely difficult to give credit and praise where it is due. There is an escape route many of us choose called justification. This takes us to dimensions where anything we do can be justified to be rewarded extra in any given situation. I did extra work so I need to be paid more is justifiable because it can be quantified and is tangible. But I deserve more because I love you more than the others is not justifiable as it is intangible.

In our lives we can choose our friends but cannot choose our family. So, we have a choice with people other than family to continue with the relationship or drop it.

Everyone likes predictable behaviour for a stable relationship. The moment the equilibrium is upset relationships get rough. So, in order to maintain a good relationship with family, friends and colleagues we need to function in the realms of the established relationship boundaries.

Are there any other classifications we need to know about relationship behaviours? The answer is Yes.

The following are behaviour patterns demonstrated.

1. Passive
2. Aggressive
3. Assertive
4. Deviant

Passive:

People who demonstrate passive behaviour are doormats who allow others to walk over them and use them. While they may allow others to do this, they resent it inwardly. When they can't take it any longer, they have an outburst which destroys the relationship. In most cases breaks it up. While they are loved by everyone because of their amiable nature they suffer a lot inside.

Aggressive

These are brash individuals who have no concern for others feelings and bulldoze their way. They are rude, demanding, selfish and inconsiderate. They are the most hated but tolerated sometimes because they are in positions of power. They usually leave a relationship because of the hostility against them or are thrown out as the other party cannot tolerate them anymore.

Assertive

It is the best form of behaviour one can demonstrate. Simply put, a person who can state his views clearly and gets acceptance or has the ability to recognize the talent of another and accepts it. These people work for the good of everyone. They are happy that each one brings to the table his own strengths for everyone's good.

Deviant

There are a series of behaviours demonstrated in this category which are hybrids of the above 4 forms.

a) **Passive Aggressive**

Here the person behaves in a passive manner but is always on the look out to bring the aggressor down and does this in his own unique way. A danger situation.

b) **Narcissist**

A person who is often double faced & has the Jekyll & Hyde syndrome. Obnoxious, cruel and a sadist on the one hand and helpful loving a great friend on the other.

c) **Stockholm Syndrome**

A person who likes the abuse of his captor and comes back repeatedly to be treated in the same way.

d) **Toxic**

Toxicity can be of two types. Where a person or persons spread negativity when you are in their company. Pulling you down, criticizing you and making you feel like a load of garbage. This type must be dropped from your life. The second type may not be your real enemy but a well-wisher. Being in their company and listening to them, however, pulls you down and lowers your state. You must spot this and steer away before it affects you, as you may not be able to drop them as they are usually old friends or family.

Looking at the behaviours we demonstrate we see the correlation with the 4 types of relationships we have in our lives.

So, this is how it can be interpreted:

- I win you lose- Aggressive, Narcissist, Toxic
- I lose you win- Passive & Stockholm syndrome
- We both lose- Passive aggressive & Toxic
- We both win-Assertive

Keeping in mind the framework for a life journey with great relationships we have to strive towards working on win-win relationships with an assertive behaviour demonstrated in all our interactions with others be it with family, friends and colleagues and with all who we come in contact.

When we view the behaviour of the people we know intimately like our family, close friends and colleagues it is baffling how their behaviour patterns change with different people. I will illustrate it with a few personal examples.

1. A person who is willing to give their life for any friend in need and very helpful, who can be approached day or night is rude and abusive with domestic staff and even gets physically violent with them.
2. A socialite who will splurge on visibility but will bargain with the vegetable vendor for a few rupees.
3. A colleague who is all sugar in front but spreads malicious gossip about you behind you back

4. A boss who preaches and makes the right politically correct statements but never practices it with his own subordinates.
5. A parent who appears successful and considered the ideal parent but is abusive in the home.
6. A child who portrays being loving and caring to the family but is the opposite in reality.
7. People who have a public façade different to what they show at home.

I am sure many of you will resonate with the above examples. Our goal should be to live our life in a manner that does not take advantage of others weaknesses and is based on integrity, fairness and trust.

Laws, Traditions, Culture and Customs came into being to give clarity & boundaries to our family relationships.
Culture, customs the unwritten code of the group, civil /religious code apply to our friend circle.
Company rules and culture with corporate, labor & other applicable laws apply to our colleagues.

So, in our country there are different laws customs, cultures & traditions which have come down over the years to foster harmonious family relationships. These are specific to regions, religion, and communities and sometimes unique to a family.

Whenever there is a disruption or a different interpretation to any of the above, relationship issues crop up and this is typical in family feuds.

Typically, these feuds end up in court with no decision taken during the life time of the litigants as courts take 20+ years to give any decision and it's only getting worse.

We need to respect family tenets to live and maintain harmonious relationships. Because what happens in the home is carried to other areas of our life and influences our behaviour with others. A few quick examples are love, integrity, honesty, respect, harmony, trust, caring, flexibility etc.

Today the structure of our culture has changed and has a new meaning- its urban, semi urban and rural with people living as nuclear families. This calls for a relook and classification of wealth distribution for the future generations but not going into the past as it will cause a lot of unpleasantness & disharmony.

Unfortunately, in many families there has always been one bad apple that starts this disharmony. It can be born out of sibling rivalry, jealousy, envy or pure greed. Fortunately, in many instances it is quashed in the bud but in some cases, it festers and ruins the very fabric of the family's existence.

If this bad apple is aggressive, passive aggressive or a narcissist one can be rest assured that the family is heading for doom. The aggressive person wants to win at any cost irrespective of the consequences it has on others. This behaviour results in 2 dimensions of our relationships either I win you lose or both lose. The worst is the Narcissist. They are scheming, devious, manipulative, cruel, abusive and obnoxious and will go to any extent to get what they want. Ruthless in their behaviour and torture those who don't fall in line with threats which they execute. They are usually well aligned with the right contacts and build for themselves a support group of people across all walks of life who further their cause. A strange phenomenon of these people is they usually have someone who suffers the Stockholm syndrome and carries out their orders and readily succumbs to their evil whims & fancies begging them for more to get their recognition. A quote that comes to mind is, "History repeats itself". From evidence it is true. Be always vigilant to see the writing on the wall before it becomes too late. Once disruptive behaviour is noticed we need to work on getting it sorted. If not done timely, the consequences become massive and at times irreversible. The efforts to put it back on an even keel will drain all your resources- physical, social, emotional, mental and financial.

I would like to leave my readers with 10 points to keep in mind to make their relationships magical, more meaningful and enriched.

1. Sort out home relationships first as it impacts the lens, we view the world though.
2. Strive towards creating win-win relationships.
3. Communication sorts out many relationship issues – keep channels open.
4. Mediate before litigation.
5. Look at the situation from a macro angle.
6. Be open minded, progressive and think positively.
7. Work towards a resolution and be a problem solver.
8. Never compromise on your values.
9. Treat others as you would like to be treated.
10. A great relationship is based on two principles. First appreciate similarities and second respect differences. You can even agree to disagree.

CHAPTER 7

Sanjali Ekatpure

Sanjali Ekatpure is an enthusiast, with boundless zest for life.

Masters in Nutrition and Dietetics. Bachelors in food technology. Food safety officer FSSAI. Music Therapist. Certified life coach.

She holds a rich experience of 16+ years in the healthcare industry as a lifestyle and nutrition consultant. She has successfully transformed the health of people with varied ailments. She aspires to treat root causes, spread happiness with ease and good health.

Join in for abundance of health transformation!!

THE NUTRITION MINDSET

Once upon a time, we lived by the rule of authority. We believed what was told and spoken around us. Now, science has become the new authority. In some cases, it saves lives. For some it remains a dilemma! Truly speaking health is a perception, what is it for you?

With all of my professional practice, learnings and newer self-research, I have questions that allow me dive deeper to help cure, thrive. It makes life meaningful. It's time for a paradigm shift. Progress doesn't happen without the very frame work being questioned.

So why live with a disease, when you can actually get rid of it? Every living being has the innate ability to heal, it's a connection to self. Life is all about possibilities, flowing……

Spiritual connect: A group of five elements is the basis of all life's creations, according to the cosmic culture. They are earth, fire, water, air and sky. Every living being is made of these components, which also represent 5 human senses. According to Ayurveda and yoga, any imbalance in these interrupts the energy chakras causing disease. Mudra therapy is used with specific fingers of hands to focus on these elements for healing. So, it's the way you believe to heal.

Are you, by any chance stagnating due to illness? Don't let this ever happen, I'm here very much reachable.

Our fast-paced lives, rapid urbanization together with convenient food choices and physical inactivity are culprits. Every human advancement has its pros and cons.

Cherry on the cake is technology, work from home and learn from home.

Nature has its own rhythm. How much do we align with it? Our circadian rhythms are natural body clocks, programmed for our metabolic activities. The more we stay in sync, the more we stay attuned with health. It simply means, wake up with the chirping of birds and sleep as early as possible, not so difficult. Isn't it?

This allows your body to function smoothly, making energy flow naturally.

Emotional Connect: As humans we experience numerous shades of emotions, rather we flow with them. Being aware of your state of mind does wonders. It might be a stress full experience or an overwhelming joy, acknowledge it. Do you ever wonder, why I'm the way I'm? We have our own core values, which help us take decisions. I have seen emotional eating disorders out of boredom, frustration, insult, failures and rejections. The story of health begins here, are you with me on this note?

Acceptance of the moment makes life meaningful. Any negative feelings, not expressed rightly invite behavioral and health issues. Have a buddy, it may be your mom, dad, sibling, friend or spouse. The one you can vent out with and celebrate too. A gratitude diary towards the end of the day or journaling in the morning is also a sound way to stay grounded to self.

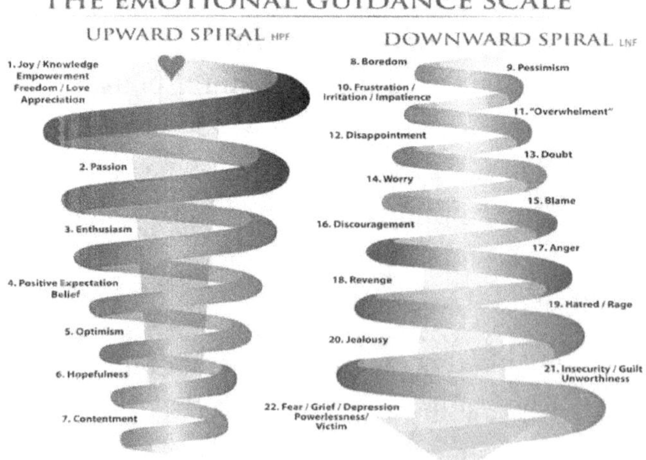

Your contribution: Cooking, which is an essential part of life is ruled by feminism since ages. It's time for us to take ownership of this skill, enjoy it. Help yourself, you know your choices better, why someone else?

Our fast-paced lives, rapid urbanization together with convenient food choices and physical inactivity make it further difficult. Cooking practices, hybrid food sources, heavy fertilization, adulteration, environment pollutants, metal toxins are all add on to altering the natural biochemical set up of body.

Endocrine systems are closely associated seven energy chakras of our body. Any imbalance in one chakra also, initiates certain signals which we need to critically identify. Time is the only asset in this universe. A dramatic change in metabolic pathways leads to much later seen disease symptoms. Here a new story begins. Treatment, guilt, pain, side effects, complications, misery.

Recent Outbreaks: Viruses are a medium to shake us up. Big players today are emotional health, stress, detachment from self, driven away with metabolic syndrome (insulin resistance, diabetes mellitus, elevated lipid profiles, hypertension, and obesity). Allergies, gut health, thyroid disorders, chronic inflammation, arthritis, skin issues all together create havoc.

Low immunity is just the hottest topic at the moment since 2020, as the newer COVID 19 strains invade humanity. So, not contracting any infection is not victory, but fighting it with good antibodies certainly is! Agree?

Immunity: This term is much like a finished product, gone through so many steps and trials. Immunity is an asset to be earned with your dedication and lifestyle. It can't be achieved overnight, with any pill or a single food.

The factors building immunity are your daily habits. It includes sound sleep routine at night, challenging exercise pattern, balanced meals, proper digestion and good elimination of wastes, stable mind, healthy relationships, work life balance and smart nutritional supplements.

Malnourishment in any way, may it be undernourished or over nourished, has to evaluate himself for nutritional status. Your hemoglobin, cell count, blood sugar levels, calcium, magnesium, Vit B12, lipid profile, kidney function tests, liver profile says it all.

Healthy body weight as per height, body fat percentage, waist circumference, BMI are anthropometry parameters to consider stringently. The Asian population is emerging into obese one, inviting all sorts of health issues. Those which actually need only self-motivation and some genuine professional help, to revert and bounce back to life.

I always have said, life is precious, handle with care. Your body is such a unique model of Audi, own it with passion and drive with care. All the safety features are in built, so does it mean you can't identify the red flags on express ways? Certainly not accepted, every model is precious.

Diet therapy: What comes to your mind, when you hear the word "Diet"? For many of us it is a non-reliable solution, seems sophisticated at times. You might think of crash diets, fad diets, protein shakes etc. Few might think of instant, quick fix pills.

The true concept of diet is focusing on eating right, the right way in right proportions. The purpose is optimum health, managing ailments, strength and fitness. What can you do, nutrition wise, to ensure you are putting forth needed efforts?

Chronic illness is at an all-time high. Just as we go closer to the modern medicine, so many people have suffered with no complete answers, which have put this progress at a toss! Either it's a gene blame game or autoimmunity, which puts the truth further away.

Treating the root cause is easy to work out, sustainable, safe. My job is to provide the answers to you. Are you ready to perceive it?

Right nutrition has the ability to correct the roadblocks of energy pathways. Various other roles are those of nourishment, protein synthesis, wear and tear, energy generation and growth.

Many have the notion as adults that they don't require any proteins, vitamins, minerals, as there is no physical growth now. But what about the productive development in life? Every cell in the body has a shelf-life, it needs nourishment and rejuvenation to keep you going. There is a process called 'Apoptosis'. The death of cells which occurs as a normal and controlled part of a human development. The very twist in this process, is seen as abnormal cell growth- tumors, ruled by genetic mutations.

At this point of time, we are abruptly changing our DNA. Isn't that the beginning of a hurricane? No wonder the healthcare sector is flourishing leaps and bounds. The only grudge, life isn't blooming with affluence. Financial stability certainly doesn't work if you do not have the zest for life.

That inner DNA, intact self is being altered, mutated with various lifestyle changes. Who can take a call on LIFE or STYLE?

Let's talk nutrition: Any food that you consume on this planet, is going to provide you nutrients. That is the definition of food. For example, *roti* is classified as carbs, as it is rich in carbohydrates.

The basic nutrients of food are macronutrients and if the food is super healthy it has good micronutrients also. This is known as an energy dense food. Macronutrients are required in larger amounts, hence the name 'macro'. Macronutrients consist of proteins, carbohydrates, fats and water. I'm sure all of you are known to their various roles in the body and how they impact our body.

A proper nutrition plan will have you eating a balanced level of each of these nutrients. Except water, macronutrients provide energy and contain calories, which is the unit of energy that the body uses for fuel. The approximate calories in the various macronutrients are as follows:

Macronutrient	Calories
Protein	4 calories/gm
Carbohydrates	4 calories/gm
Fats	9 calories/gm

As we see, fat provides more than twice the energy from proteins and carbohydrates. So, we need to take it in restricted amounts. Eating healthy food is just not enough, if you are looking at weight control. You need to look into right amount of healthy food.

Two other important foods that generate calories are alcohol and insoluble fiber. Alcohol provides empty calories, as much as 7 calories/gm, without any vital micronutrients. This is one reason why consuming alcohol regularly can set you up for fat gain, elevated lipid profile and central body obesity. Your liver is all over burdened with detoxifying, ultimately the energy pathways are hampered.

It weakens the will power to eat healthy foods, causing irreversible neurological impact. Protein synthesis is also hampered.

People ask for options, like which type of alcohol is good to be taken occasionally. My answer is, are there types of poison? If it is non-essential and still you take, it causes a gradual increase in threshold. This unknowingly raises your limitations, a step towards addiction.

Insoluble fiber is a form of carbohydrate that doesn't get fully digested in the body, but helps the elimination of wastes from the gut. 1gm of dietary fiber provides only 2 calories, hence diets rich in fiber help in weight control.

Next, we have micronutrients that don't provide any energy, but serve a wide array of important functions. They are required in small doses, called as vitamins and minerals. All nutrient dense foods are rich in these micronutrients. You are at a greater risk of having deficiencies of micros, when you are not eating healthy foods. A diet for example, highly processed in fats and sugars is devoid of these vital micronutrients. Junk foods, carbonated beverages, shakes, pastries, bakery products, milk sweets, etc.

On a contrary, someone who eats a diet rich in fresh fruits, vegetables, lean proteins, whole grains and legumes, healthy nuts and seeds, oil in very small portions, provides proper nourishment. That's exactly why you need to pay attention to not only how much food to eat, but type of food is also to be considered.

Our relationship with food, mood at the time of consuming a meal, speed of eating, also has a relevance in nutritional history. The key to many digestive issues and insulin resistance lies here. Mindfulness during meal times helps us enjoy food with the virtue to energize the body, providing satiety.

Sources of raw ingredients, vegetables, seasonal fruits, milk, chicken, eggs, fish are also equally important. Be inquisitive, for organic, whole varieties of grains (with husk and vitamins), fruits without artificial ripening, fortified milk products, fresh water fish(free from toxic metals) etc. Storage of foods at optimal temperatures, like being vigilant about internal temperature of refrigerator helps to categorize zones for perishable products.

Dry grocery also needs smart storage to avoid food infestations. Any packet foods must be chosen only after reading food labels. Sodium, trans fats, simple sugars, colors, preservatives are all health hazards, in a way causing hormonal, growth and metabolic issues in all age groups. Children being the worst hit of all.

Conventionally we had our elaborate cooking recipes, hand grounded masalas, local veggies, slow cooking methods on *Chulha* that actually happened with an extra touch of love.

Compassion is missing today, with availability of time, money and home food delivery apps. So much knowledge on media about food, nutrition and health, which goes unapplied on a daily basis. We need to get back, plan our menu wisely for taste, health and a better planet.

Food waste needs a stringent approach though, and can be channelized in a proper way.

Water:

Our body is composed of 75% water. Every cell communicates and functions with hydration. Have you thought, why do you get a headache after a travel without enough water intake?

Hydration helps both, digestion and detoxification. Good 8-10 glasses of water is a healthy adult's water requirement of the day. Other fluids like buttermilk, coconut water, lemon water, soups, and juices can be consumed. Avoid adding simple sugars to drinks. More than 2 cups of tea or coffee have dehydrating effects, pulling out water from the body.

Ask yourself daily, how much water have I consumed? Easy, right?

Proteins:

To elaborate, proteins are the building blocks of our body, made up of various amino acids. Plant proteins are rich in branch chain amino acids, easy for assimilation in the body. Animal proteins on the other hand are complete packages, ready to use.

How much protein per day? It all depends on the age, physiological stage (growth, pregnancy etc.) health status and physical activity. Generally, 1 gm/kg body weight for a healthy adult is the requirement. They provide satiety, have high thermal effect of food and regulate blood sugar levels. That makes proteins a buzz macro-nutrient for all the age groups.

Carbohydrates: Going off carbs is recent trend these days, as there is lot of confusion around intake of carbohydrates. This is not true for every person. For example, an athlete would require more carbs than an average sedentary person.

The traditional Indian cuisine, may it be extreme north or extreme south, has a dominance of carbohydrates. Types of carbohydrates is a topic of self-learning. A meticulous overall calorie calculation helps to give right requirements.

After digestion, carbohydrates are broken down to smaller glucose molecules. The speed at which those carbohydrates are broken down and glucose is released into the bloodstream will all depend on:

1. The type of carbohydrate you eat (sugar or spinach)

2. How much carbohydrate is eaten (a bar of chocolate or a piece of chocolate)

3. Other combination of macronutrient (a vegetable sandwich or egg sandwich)

4. Processing / cooking method used (instant noodles or overcooking)

5. Drinks/juices with sugars or without sugar

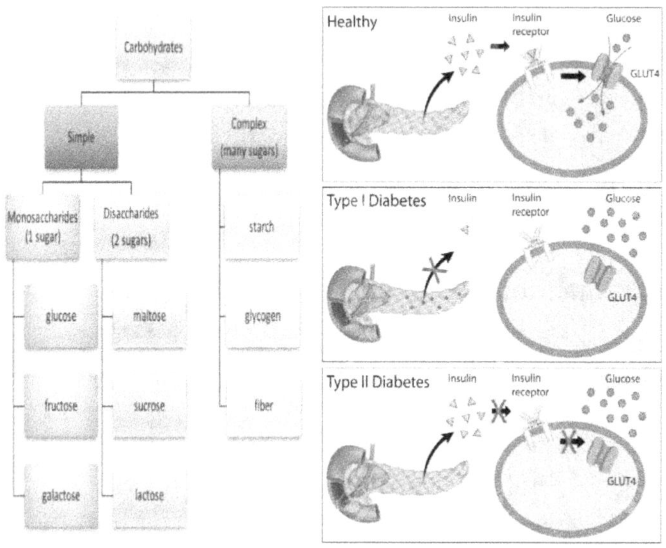

Types of carbs are complex, simple and fibers depending on their structures and glycemic index. Hormone insulin is released from the pancreas after every meal, to help the body cells utilize glucose effectively. There are also other counter regulatory hormones working to maintain a balance for blood sugar levels. Types of carbohydrates: Insulin action in glucose uptake.

Role of Carbohydrates- This macro has many reasons why you should be eating carbs in right portions.

A. They are primary energy providing nutrient, which keep us going with activity. A steady supply from your diet is a must. All fad diets claiming low carb meals are only meant for defined small periods, as they have their own ill effects.

B. Secondly, carbs help you sustain a proper metabolic rate. It works with hormone leptin to control your hunger pangs and maintain satiety, keeping crazy cravings at bay!

C. Rest functions include regular bowel movements, proper brain functions and muscle mass building.

Fruits are special type of carbohydrates with dietary fiber, which slows the release of glucose into blood stream. They are loaded with antioxidants, vitamins and minerals. 2 seasonal fruits per day, at mid meal times is ideal for healthy individuals. Consume them with skin for complete nutritional benefits. Avoid taking juices and shakes with added simple sugars.

Fruits - Sources of dietary fiber

Dietary fibers help to delay the emptying of stomach, which creates greater sense of fullness after eating a meal, helping reduce hunger pangs and managing blood glucose levels. Other benefits of fiber are it controls the pH within the gastrointestinal tract, binds excess cholesterol and toxins and eases the process of elimination via bowels. As per guidelines by ICMR, daily fiber requirement for every 1000calorie diet is 12gm. This accounts for about 25-30gms/day, in sync with gender and calorie intake.

Whole grains, beans, lentils, peas, dals with skin, psyllium husk, flaxseed, orange, guava, mangoe, lady finger, drumstick, broccoli, sweet potato, apricot are some of the valuable sources of fiber.

Need some help to boost your fiber intake?

1. Begin your day with bran cereal or oatmeal, combined with veggies.

2. Always eat fruits with skin.

3. Choose raw vegetables and fruits as a quick snack on the go, during work or travel.

4. Go vegetarian at least 2 days a week to increase your fiber intake.

5. Start your meal with a bowl of salads.

6. Add mixed seeds on salads, chutneys, dips and raitas.

7. Smoothies are another power packed combo for great benefits.

8. For dinners make stir-fry/sautéed veggies or clear veg soups.

Dietary Fats and Oils:

These are packed with calories, in our daily meals in the form of oil, ghee, butter, nuts, and seeds. Fats are also provided from animal sources like milk, mutton, fatty fish, eggs. The type and variety of fats decides the level of inflammation in the body. Hence, we need to make a wise choice. Double filtered vegetable oils are known to have natural phytosterols intact, which make them a better choice.

On the other hand, fried foods are harmful due to the production of trans-fats. Bakery, junk and processed foods are hence in the forbidden list of foods.

Functions of fats: Fats are carriers of fat-soluble vitamins, hormone production, blood sugar regulation and providing reserve energy stores.

Vital Micronutrients: Micronutrients are the less spoken about, driving force of a balanced diet. They comprise of all vitamins and minerals, involved in hundreds of biochemical cycles in the body.

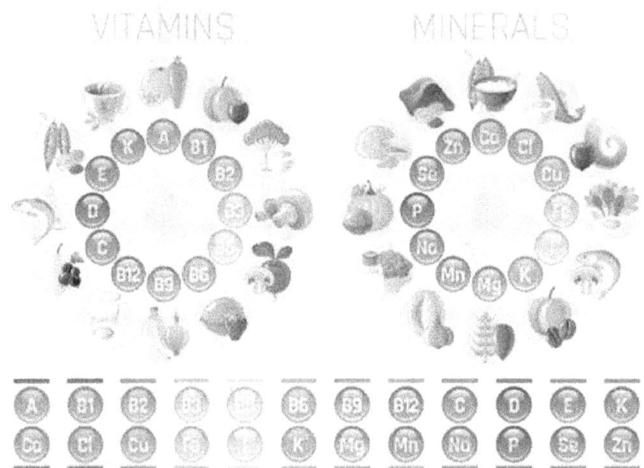

All energy pathways and detoxification processes are dependent on these tiny units. They are precursors to many vital units and catalyze reactions smoothly.

In a way, they are the soul of nutrition science.

Hence, these stores need daily replenishment through good food, water and smart supplements. Professional advice gives you a clear picture about how much and when to take supplements.

Physical activity:

It won't be an exaggeration to say, "Nothing goes right without physical activity"! Simply moving is life. Exercise must be an inevitable part of every age group. It activates metabolic pathways, governs energy production and limits fat deposition.

We are now confined to closed work places, sedentary work. But simple solutions of choosing stairs over elevators is the need of the hour. Going for a walk for 30 minutes in a day and then being a couch potato for 23.30 hours can't serve the purpose. Remain active throughout, it's a sign of liveliness.

If you were walking, try intermittent jogging. Make a challenging combo of cardio, weights and floor abs. Set your health goals with conviction. The more muscle in your body, higher is your metabolic rate!

This is the key to healthy aging. There's nothing wrong in this quest of being fit and young. You take the ownership of health. The ball is in your court!

Let us join the drive of living life to the fullest with your complete commitment and I will help you achieve your dream goals.

If you are dealing with a health challenge, the storm will pass. Finding peace within you, will come with your free fill.

Let health prevail, with abundance.

CHAPTER 8

Sunita Kulkarnee

Sunita Kulkarnee, is a Dentist by profession with 27 years of experience in teaching and administration. This is her 3rd book as an author. She has been an avid networker with efficiency and experience in public speaking. She is passionate about fitness and diet control and great at sprucing herself up within 10 minutes. She is talented and has various hobbies like singing, cooking, gardening, painting and drawing.

She has an earnest desire to impact lives of people, by helping them to inculcate a sense of discipline towards diet, working out and grooming.

EXERCISE AND GROOMING

A) EXERCISE:

It was in around the year 2016, I was getting ready for an informal outing, when I noticed that the top that used to flaunt my flat wash-board like abs, suddenly started projecting a paunch. I was shocked and I casually weighed myself, and to my surprise I was 64kgs. This was overweight by my standard and I panicked. I was 52 years at that time and for some it could be fine, but I could be happy with much less. I was reading a book by a famous dietician and she quite emphatically mentioned that it was a good idea to join a gym and do workout about 4 times a week.

I was quite into exercising and yoga since 2002, had joined various gyms and was into regular workouts. But now the motivation was much bigger and I joined a very good gym and my love affair with workouts began.

Exercise is as important as eating food daily. Whether you are thin or fat, young or old, even for children, physical activity is a must.

Ask yourself certain questions. Do I exercise? If no, then why not? Is it a good practice? Should I start as soon as possible? How will it help me? What if you can get a great strategy that truly inspires you to start exercising, how will it be? Write in detail about everything you can think about working out. You will find out solutions.

It is said that proper nourishment and the right dose of exercise can keep mankind healthy and fit. Any deficiency in these two areas can make people sick.

It keeps the lungs, liver, kidneys, and other organs in great shape. It strengthens the heart, so let us keep it pumping folks. Controls the blood pressure and keeps cholesterol in check. Improves immunity and prevents chronic diseases. Obesity and type II diabetes are controlled and kept in check.

It prevents cancer of the breast and colon.

It keeps the muscles and bones strong.

In adults and children, keeps depression away. It reduces anxiety and stress, increases the ability to deal with stressful situations in a better manner.

Increases the blood flow to the brain, helps it to absorb the nutrients and oxygen in an effective way and, thus improves attention and memory functions.

Moving the body, increases the power of the brain thus increasing creative thinking and giving super ideas.

It elevates mood and vitality, giving a feeling of well-being. Doing Aerobics is so fantastic that it increases serotonin secretion and other neurotransmitters, helping people to feel happy and ecstatic. This naturally can help anyone to look and feel young.

Our body has a musculoskeletal system and we need to move our body systematically to remain fit and young forever. The heart is also a muscle and we need to keep it in great shape.

It increases alertness and concentration, which can help us achieve so much more, ultimately giving us a feeling of satisfaction and indirectly helping us to feel young and youthful.

The diet helps you to lose weight but exercising will tone your body and help you to lose inches. If you have stubborn fat and you are overweight, exercise is a must. Please don't get fooled by people telling you that with no exercise weight loss can be achieved. You will find some advertisements promoting that. It will be better not to fall into that trap.

I can assure you that exercise gives more happiness than money. We cannot predict our longevity, but one thing is sure that either you can be in great health and enjoy the life span that we are destined to have and live a happy, healthy life, instead of spending it with ill health and compromised state of mind and looks.

If done sincerely, the satisfaction one could derive is beyond description. The sweating removes all the toxins and the lightness you feel gives a feeling of euphoria.

When we workout, the sweat, the body stretching and twisting, running, cycling, makes you feel euphoric because it releases endorphins which is a feel-good hormone and helps to get rid of all tensions and gives a feeling of elation.

In women especially, it keeps the hormonal system in balance.

It is not necessary to lose too much weight, as it can make you lose muscle mass, and your face may lose the charm making you look haggard. But with the same weight, you can look fat or thin. It is about the loss of inches, and proper diet and exercise can give you a fantastic figure and help you to look fit and fresh.

One can start with just about 15-20 minutes in the beginning if you are a reluctant candidate. Simple stretching while watching TV, especially during commercial breaks, learning exercises that can be done while sitting can help you get into the full mode of working out gradually, but after a particular age the fat becomes stubborn, and heavy diet and lack of exercise can make things a bit difficult in terms of weight and inch loss.

I will give you a good mantra to get up and start exercising if you are one of those who just can't get yourself to start a regimen. Some may be very busy and have very little time, but many are simply reluctant to take the first step. It is important to take out half an hour per day for our well-being.

The best thing is to start collecting the exercise gear for yourself. Go shopping and buy bright and cheerful tee-shirts and tights. Buy very good quality shoes. The retail therapy will motivate you to begin your daily routine.

On day one, wear the entire outfit and see how it feels. Sometimes it is just the inertia to don the workout gear that prevents us from getting into a regimen. Do this activity for two days, even if you don't start exercising. After, about two to three days of doing so, you will automatically start getting into the mode. On the third day wear your outfit and begin with some stretching. You can go out of the house and walk for 15 minutes. That's it! I can guarantee that you can easily slip into the routine with this technique and once you start, there is no looking back, so addictive the workout routine can be.

Wearing a nice bright gear can motivate you to workout.

Regimen: One should always begin with a warm-up. It prepares your body for an extensive regimen.

WARMUP: One can start with neck extensions, jack knives, jumping or jogging in place, leg and arm rotations, and stretching which is excellent form of exercise.

FLOOR EXERCISES: They are highly effective and you can target specific body parts like the upper and lower abs, love handles, arms, the lower body that includes the waist, hips and, lower extremities. Systematic targeting of these areas can help you burn the stubborn fat accumulated especially for those above 40 years.

ISOLATION EXERCISES:

1)Upper abs: There are various exercises like abs crunches, butterfly crunches, half or full push-ups, elbow planks, which is a complete exercise in itself, stomach vacuum for targeting the deeper abs, lying on your back and doing leg rotations are some effective exercises for the upper abs.

2) Waist or love handles area: Trikonasana, weighted side crunches, hip-dips and ardha-matsyendrasana, will help to melt the love-handles.

3) Hips: Standing position side leg raises, doggie position leg rotations, weighted squats, elbow prop with legs extended sideways at 45degree angle and doing unilateral clockwise and anti-clockwise cycling movements are very effective to reduce the hips.

4) Lower Abs: Reverse crunches, mountain climbers, scissors kicks and weighted squats will help to get rid of the lower belly pooch.

5)Arms: Arm rotations, roof raisers, walnut crusher arm extension, weighted arm raises and reverse plank, can give excellent results in toning your arms.

6) Lower body: Unilateral leg swings, support squats with several repetitions, leg lunges and stepper jumps can give you a very slim and toned lower body.

Now that you know some of the isolation exercises, I will suggest a regimen that you can create for yourself and start with 45 minutes in the beginning and gradually work out to a routine of around one to one and a half hour daily.

REGIMEN:

1) Start your routine with a warm-up for 5-10 minutes.

2) Decide which areas you would like to target, and select three parts and do a combination of two exercises for each area for 10 minutes. So, three areas will take 30 minutes. It is up to you, as to how many areas you would like to target in a day.

3) Once you complete this routine, you can go for a fast walk for 20 to 30 minutes. Once you start walking, you can upgrade to spurts of running, and walking alternately, which also can become a type of high-intensity interval training (HIIT). You can find out details of this on the internet and is very interesting. It suggests, that a high-intensity

interval workout increases the heart rate which helps burn calories.

4) Cycling is a fantastic alternative because you have to do it outdoors and as you can see people; it tends to be less boring.

5) If you feel lazy to go out, do skipping for 10 minutes. There are numerous benefits of doing this for 10 minutes.

6) After an intense workout, let your body cool down for 10 minutes.

B) GROOMING:

Get ready for an exciting journey from hair to toe, so that you can maintain every part of the body that will make you look so much younger and smarter and you will learn a lot about taking care of important aspects of your beautiful body.

HAIR:

Well-groomed hair adds oodles to your personality, and, you will agree that it can make you look good or bad! That's how important hair grooming is!

Whatever hair type you have, it must look well-groomed and there are so many styles you can learn. Two very important tools you must possess is a good quality iron or hairbrush which runs on electricity and heats and straightens your hair in minutes. There is no need for poker-straight hair.

However, it should be used so that your hair becomes manageable and you can style it decently. A very important aspect is the grey hair popping its ugly head and giving an un-even, and shabby look. I would advise you to take care of it urgently with very good quality hair colour, which takes hardly half an hour to do the routine. It will take away years off your face, making you look young and fresh.

FACE:

Your face says it all. If you have a bright, happy, smiling face you are done. You simply can't look old. I shall categorize different parts of the face and shall discuss how to take care of each part.

1) SKIN:

Skin of the face and of course in general says it all. It is a great indicator of your health status. Beautiful, smooth shining, vibrant skin adds stars to your personality, and having beautiful skin can take years off your face and help you to look youthful.

Adequate hydration, a proper diet, avoiding junk food, aerated drinks, and good sleep with a healthy lifestyle will keep your skin naturally wonderful. But we cannot take our skin for granted.

SKIN CARE ROUTINE:

It involves cleansing, scrubbing, toning, mask application and moisturizing. This regimen should be followed at-least thrice weekly to keep your skin looking fresh and glowing and will help in anti-ageing. One must always use sunscreens daily. It is said that it is a good practice to use sunscreen even at home! That is how bad the ultraviolet rays can be.

MAKEUP:

The first thing that hits us when we hear about makeup is the heavily plastered kind of makeup. It may not be so always. It can also be very light makeup and can transform your face in minutes.

It will be a good idea to learn the art of makeup, which can come in very handy. It's important to use the foundation, concealer, powder, blush-on, kajal, eye-shadow and eyeliner in a professional manner so that it looks decent. I am an ardent lipstick fan and it can brighten the face in seconds.

Close-up of elaborate, yet subtle makeup which can light up your face

Men have skin too! Nowadays there are skin care products, especially for men. Though it will be too much to ask of them to use make-up for work place, but during socializing and for parties or other special events, it can be a good practice to get used to it. Minimalistic approach is the best to look good, and maintain the subtlety.

2) EYEBROWS:

Beautifully arched, thick, and dark eyebrows nicely maintained and cleaned off the extra hair can add oomph to your face. Even men are getting conscious about getting their eyebrows trimmed. I have observed that in the unisex salons, that has become the in thing nowadays.

Dark eyebrows look very good and add a nice dimension to the face. I will tell you very natural ways to get them.

Aloe vera gel and castor oil applied just before sleeping can give you 3 shades dark eyebrows within a week. A combination of vitamin E oil, castor oil and coconut oil application, is a fantastic natural way to get dark and thick eyebrows.

3) EYELASHES:

Everybody loves long, thick, and dark eyelashes.

What an amazing difference, beautiful eyelashes make to a face. It is a common observation that the film stars or the T.V actors, use light makeup but consistently use false eyelashes for the dramatic look.

Get long, thick, beautiful lashes with most natural way. Coconut oil applied liberally before sleeping, castor oil also applied similarly gives amazing results. You will be able to see them growing. Another good way is to use egg white mask. Gently apply with ear buds and let it dry for half an hour and then wash off with warm water.

4) EYES:

The eyes are the most expressive and beautiful part of the face. They speak volumes without a sound. It is so important to take care of the eyes and protect them from any harm.

Some important tips to keep your eyes healthy:

Eat well, especially green leafy vegetables, fish, nuts, oranges and vitamin C. Quitting smoking and wearing sun-glasses will go a long way to protect the delicate eyes.

5) LIPS:

Beautiful, luscious, pink lips can hide your age and you can look lovely and youthful.

Dry, flaky lips tend to reduce aesthetics and can make you feel uncomfortable. So, here are a few tips to have nice, soft pink lips forever.1tsp each of almond oil and honey and lightly ground sugar, because if the crystals are bigger, can be harsh on the lips. Mix all the ingredients and gently scrub your lips, to remove the dead cell and the oil and honey will moisturize the delicate skin.

Lip balm with SPF 15 can help damage from the sun and help prevent pigmentation of the delicate skin.

 Moisturize regularly with available gentle moisturizers. You can take a fresh aloe vera leaf and use the gel directly on your lips, which can be super beneficial.

For those who are very particular about not using any artificial products, lipsticks can be replaced with natural tints like the juice of pomegranate, beetroot, or raspberry. They will give you beautiful rosy lips, at the same time keeping them moisturized and healthy.

6) HANDS:

Let us go to the very important part of our body, which is, our hands. They are constantly working and need to be taken care of. Neatly maintained hands are very important as they are being noticed by everyone. I am of a strong belief that rather than for others, we should take care for ourselves, for a sense of well-being. If we feel good about ourselves, we can conquer the world.

Properly clipped or maintained nails and regularly moisturizing the hand can make them look very good.

However, getting it done in a salon can be so expensive and for no reason. You can have a luxurious routine at home for just a dime and at your convenience.

1) The first step is to remove the nail polish if you have applied it before. A non-acetone-based remover would be better, but you can use one of your choice. I would suggest going for good brands because cheaper ones can discolour the nails.

2) You can clip or shape your nails by gently filing them. Instead of metal, use an emery board or crystal nail files.

3) Gently buff your nails, but not too much or the nail polish may get difficult to be applied.

4) Soaking: The most luxurious part of the routine is to soak your hands. Warm water is ideal. There are many combinations that you can use for soaking. Just add a gentle shampoo, little baking soda, and a piece of lemon.

If you can get your hands on essential oils, the fragrance will be relaxing, and they are very good to make your hands soft as cotton. You can add a little drama by putting some rose petals, which will make you feel like a queen! Soak for about 5 minutes. With a nice soft brush, cleanse your hands till the elbow. The beautiful foam of the shampoo and the cleansing and whitening effect of the sweet soda will leave your hands looking fresh and glowing.

5) Then push your cuticles carefully without hurting yourself. These will make your nails look well defined and big.

6) With a cuticle remover gently remove the cuticle that will give a clean look to the nails.

7) Now is the time to scrub. I will suggest coffee powder which is rich in minerals and antioxidants and makes your skin look white and glowing.

Mix it with coconut oil to get a thick paste and gently scrub your hands, giving a little more pressure at the elbows to reduce the darkness. You will feel an instant glow and will give a squeaky-clean feeling. Some mint or other scented crystals are also available and you can use that to scrub your hands.

Besan (chick pea powder), rice powder, and a little fine brown sugar also make an excellent scrub.

8) Gently with warm water, clean the scrub off your hands and wipe dry with a towel or napkin.

9) Now comes the great part of moisturizing. You can use any, body lotion, or cream and in women's shops, you will find a big jar of moisturizer used in parlours that are beautifully scented and have a nice effect, and lasts for months. It is very affordable. You have to massage your hands lovingly till the entire cream gets absorbed into your skin.

10) The last part is applying a pack or bleaching. One can go for natural packs or use a bleaching kit available in the market and apply to the hands and keep for 15-20 minutes and then wash off.

In homemade packs, you can use a combination of rice powder, curd, and a pinch of turmeric. Mix it well and apply to your entire hand till the elbow and leave till dry. Then wash it off.

One very effective pack would be coffee powder and a tbsp of honey. Mix it well and apply liberally to the hands and keep it for 15-20 minutes and then wash off.

11) After washing your hands, again apply a layer of moisturizer and you have a beautiful manicure done.

12) Last part would be applying nail polish if you wish to. Apply a thin first coat, let it dry and then apply the second coat and you are set with beautiful glowing shining pair of hands that will make you feel rejuvenated and so young.

7) FEET:

Have you ever noticed that people generally sum you up from head to toe and some have the habit of looking at your feet glaringly? Some people judge a person and his/her personality by the way they take care of the feet. Cracked heels, unkempt nails, partly chipped, and notso aesthetic state of your nail polish, may not create a favourable impression about you.

Take care of your feet, by clipping your nails and maintaining them. Apply moisturizer regularly at night, to have nice soft feet. There are very good foot creams available which can be used regularly at least once a day for good healthy and clean pair of feet.

While having a bath at least thrice a week scrub your feet with a scraper and buff it for smoothness.

8) THE GRAND FINALE:

I hope you enjoyed the journey of sprucing yourselves up from head to toe. Now comes the time of final presentation. Whether you are going for work or for socializing, what attire you don is also an important aspect. For work it has to be something formal yet fun.

Men look good in the shirt and trousers. They too have very nice and bright colours to choose from. Wear well ironed clothes. Whatever you possess,  just take care to wear it with aplomb. Designer clothes do make a difference, but who cares? If you wear your attire with attitude, even the ordinary becomes designer. For informal wear, jeans and tee-shirt look good. Team it up with a blazer and there you go, looking your dapper self. For special occasions nowadays, even men have colourful and blingy options in clothes. Go for it and rock the world!

For women, sky is the limit. Saris make women look beautiful. There can be no apparel better than it. Take care to team it up with classily designed blouses and there you go. They can look good for formal as well as special occasions. You can don the traditional salwar or churidar-kurta combo. This also can be designed in such a way that it looks stylish, rather than mediocre. Jeans and a smart top or tee-shirtlook good on women. For work, shirt and trouser with a light weight blazer can look smart and create a good impression. I am sharing a picture of myself, wearing a sari at work. You can get an idea as to how, simplicity can be effective to create a certain impression at work.

Properly worn sari at work can create the right impact (2020)

For special occasions you have a riot of choices. Whatever you choose to wear, take care to team it up with accessories and good foot wear. Everything has to be taken care of, right from hair, makeup, the way you wear your clothes with confidence and carry them off with an attitude. I am sharing a picture of casual wear, while socializing with friends. You have to make every occasion special with the way you present yourself.

Light makeup and a simple dress is all you need to light up the atmosphere (2018)

However expensive an outfit is, if the fit is not proper and you don't have the self-confidence, it can fall flat.

In all the photographs that I have shared till now, the apparels have cost me a modest amount. I firmly believe that the choice, and the fit is most important. The way you carry it can give a moderately costing garment, a very good look.

The last but not the least, make sure that you exude a lovely fragrance always. Both men and women have a wide range of lovely perfumes and deodorants, and one should make it a point to use it to your best advantage. I am a die-hard perfume fanatic since my younger days. I do not feel complete, without a mist of lovely scent to finish off my final presentation for the day. I have always been complimented on my choice of perfumes and it creates a positive aura about you.

Now that you are well equipped, go all out and conquer the world.

CHAPTER 9

Sunita Menon

Sunitha Menon teaches, coaches, speaks & lives with conviction that happiness is achievable if we desire the same and are motivated to work towards the same. Today, she focuses on sharing these experiences through her work as a Arfeen Khan certified Life Coach, as an Author and as an Empowerment Speaker.

She holds a Master's Degree in Commerce. She is a homemaker who ran a Playschool for toddlers.

She offers consultancy to students in pursuing a career of their choice, and advises them on the various options available.

A mother of two teenagers, she presently lives in Dammam, Saudi Arabia.

HAPPINESS
A MATTER OF CHOICE

"Happiness depends on what you can give, not on what you can get"   - Swami Chinmayanada

I love cooking and take this opportunity to share my recipe for long lasting happiness.

Before getting into the ingredients let me enlighten you on how I stumbled upon this.

This recipe evolved in my college going days and has its roots in the events that occurred during my childhood.

I grew up in a loving home with good parenting and imbibed the fine virtues of a bonding family.

Personally, I was a rather shy, introvert kid. Like any child I went through a gamut of experiences.

Realization: -

I went to college and noticed that some irrelevant incidents were affecting me positively. A college mate inviting me for a get together, thanked for helping a mate with their assignment, receiving praises for performing well at an athletic meet, etc. I realized that dwelling on that incident for some time approx. 10 to 15 seconds lead to a feeling of good thoughts.

This became an unwritten rule for me and consciously practiced pushing myself to dwell on good thoughts. Now after numerous years I realized that "I was not changing my mental state, I was changing my thought process"

Mind can change the brain to change the mind. Knowing this is very important.

Our brains are funny organs. They always want whatever it is they don't have. For example, you may feel that you are unhappy due to lack of wealth, material goods, bad relationships, etc.

We are all bombarded with lots of stress, unpleasant events, negative thoughts, etc. We are all struggling with over lives in day-to-day basis. We have to handle negative workspaces, toxic persons, etc.

I am now going to take the opportunity to share with you a little secret. Nobody can make you happy or unhappy, that is up to you.

Happiness from External factors i.e. Money from lottery ticket, Gifts, false praises, etc. do not last. Happiness comes only when you feel you are worth it and earned it.

To find happiness we just need to look around us. Small bubbles of happiness exist in the chirping of birds, morning dew drops, blossoming of flowers.

Happy people do not have the best of everything, they just make the best of everything they have.

There is only one person who can make you happy & that is YOU.

Ingredients needed:

It may not seem easy, but if you will follow the tips below, you will learn to achieve long and lasting happiness. Let's start with the Ingredients in your recipe:

1. <u>You.</u>
"Happiness is when what you think, what you say, and what you do are in harmony."- Mahatma Gandhi.

Your happiness doesn't start from other people. No one can make you less happy but you. So, you have to stop relying on others to make you happy. If a person is truly happy with who they are and as they are, they don't need to have the validation from anyone.

2. <u>Be Awesome.</u>
"Have the courage to follow your heart and intuition. They somehow know what you truly want to become."- Steve Jobs

Other people will feel if you're uncomfortable with yourself. Remember that you are unique and outstanding. You have something in you that others don't have, something that you can share with others to help the world become a better place to live. If you feel good about yourself, you will begin to see the world in a different perspective and you will feel happier about it.

3. <u>Respect.</u>
"Respect yourself and others will respect you."
- Confucius

Ignore the negative aspects of your life. If you want to be able to genuinely love yourself, you have to learn how to respect yourself. Keep in mind that you're human. You will find it hard to believe in your abilities and skills. But if you look at your wonderful side, you will value yourself highly and begin to respect the person that you have become.

4. <u>Self-Appreciation.</u>
"The best things in life are yours, if you can appreciate yourself."- Dale Carniege
There is no better way to feel good from within than to appreciate your own personality. If you believe in yourself, you can do greater things. Accept that you can't be perfect, but don't stay in mediocrity. Always strive to be better, and have the attitude that you are on a journey. Work out to become the best of who you are until you learn to love yourself just the way you are.

5. <u>Motivation.</u>
"A leader is an average everyday person who is highly Motivated"- Theodere Roosevelt
Don't give up when the going gets tough. If you keep on pressing on, you will end up victorious. Motivate yourself to keep on living. Don't be afraid to tell yourself that you are doing a good job.

6. <u>Ambition.</u>
"Criticism is the price of ambition."
- Robin S Sharma
It is sweet to beloved. Furthermore, it feels good to be admired and cared for. When you care about yourself and like yourself, it will show to the world and you will feel a lot better about yourself.

7. <u>Fitness.</u>
"Take care of your body. Its the only place you have to live."-Jim Rohn
There are many physical activities that are helpful and fun at the same time. Choose an exercise according to your taste. For example, instead of running every day, go swimming during the weekends. Do some   Breathing exercises, mind relaxing meditation, etc.

8. <u>Passion</u>
"Passion is energy. Feel the power that comes from focusing on what excites you."– Oprah Winfrey
Doing something that you are passionate about is one of the best things that you can ever enjoy in your life. Imagine living your life very day, doing the things that you love. You can never be happier than that. It simply is the best life to live!

Singing, Dancing, Cooking, Baking, Painting, Writing, learning new technologies, being humorous. Just find what interests you. Including them in your daily routine will be a

Game Changer.

Can I promise you 100 percent that everything in this article will work for you? No, I can't promise that, but based on what I have seen and witnessed I do believe that its message will help you live a happier and better life.

Avoidable Ingredients:

Let's go through the Ingredients to avoid in your kitchen cupboard i.e. the areas to be avoided in your quest to be happy

1.   <u>The past</u>
"One problem with gazing too frequently into the past is that we may turn around to find the future has run out on us."– Michael Cibenko.

It's not easy to go from perceiving yourself as a victim to deciding that you have the power to do something about your life. It's not easy to accept the fact that people mistreated you and that you were deprived of love, happiness and affection.

Do it, and your life will before veterans formed and good things will start happening to you, because of you. Your past doesn't have to equally our future, unless you want it to.

2. <u>Fears.</u>
"Don't give into your fears. If you do, you won't be able to talk to your heart."-Paulo Coelho
If you want to be happy, if you want to experience them any wonders of life, and if you want to feel what it really feels like to be fully alive, you have to let go of fear.

Each day presents us with a new beginning-the opportunity to create something new, something better. To be born again and to remember who we truly are underneath all our fears, doubts and insecurities.

Don't let the troubles of yesterday occupy your mind today. Forget about your past fears, forget about yesterday's worries and make room in your heart for love. Put your past fears aside. Die to the past each night and allow yourself to be born again next morning.

Be led by your hopes, dreams and aspirations, not by your fears, problems and in securities.

3. <u>Limiting Beliefs.</u>
"It's not the events of our lives that shape us, but our beliefs as to what those events mean."-Tony Robbins
Beliefs become self-fulfilling prophecies. They shape our reality; they make us who we are. And if we really want to create a better life for ourselves and for those we love, we have to make sure that the beliefs we hold on to are serving us well and that they aren't sabotaging our happiness, health and well-being.

It can be so easy to fall into the trap of believing that who you are, is not good enough, smart enough or deserving enough.

We create our lives with our thoughts. We shape our lives based on the beliefs we have. Life gives you the things, people and experiences you feel worthy and deserving of receiving. Life treats you the way you expect to be treated; the way you believe you deserve to be treated.

Change the quality of your beliefs and the quality of your life will change too.

4. <u>Excuses.</u>
"Hold yourself responsible for a higher standard than anyone else expects of you. Never excuse yourself."-Henry Ward Beecher

A lot of times we limit ourselves because of the

many excuses we use. Instead of growing and working on improving ourselves and our lives, we get stuck, lying to ourselves, using all kinds of excuses. Excuses that 99.9 percent of the time are not even real.

We fall into the trap of thinking that we don't have enough time to do the things we want to do,that we're not ready to take the necessary steps that will contribute to our growth and happiness, that nobody will help and support us, that we don't have the necessary resources, knowledge, time and so on. And because of our attachment to all of these excuses and limitations we sell ourselves short, settling for way less than we are worth and living a life that is not ours to live.

5. <u>Resistance to change.</u>
"We delight in the beauty of the butterfly, but rarely admit the changes it has gone through to achieve that beauty."-Maya Angelou
We are creatures of habit. Most of us live our lives on auto-pilot, allowing our old programming, our past fears, excuses and limitations, to run, craft and shape our lives. And because we desperately try to keep things from changing and because we desperately try to keep life from taking it's natural course, we inflict a lot of unnecessary pain on ourselves and on those we love.

Life is meant to be fully experienced, with good and bad, with both ups and downs, and the more you try to keep life from happening by resisting and fighting change, the more you will continue to suffer and the unhappier your life will get.

Change is a natural process. You can't run away from it, just as you can't run away from life. And if you try, you'll miss out on life and you'll miss out on the great opportunity to know yourself, to be yourself and to love yourself.

6. <u>Blaming.</u>
"We are taught you must blame your father, your sisters, your brothers, the school, the teachers—but never blame yourself. It's never your fault. But it's always your fault, because if you wanted to change, you're the one who has got to change."
—Kathrine Hepburn

There is no peace in pointing the finger and making others responsible for how you feel and for what your life looks like. There is no peace in giving your power away to forces outside of yourself and making them responsible for the quality of your life. There is no peace in putting your life in other people's hands and expecting them to live it for you.

Blaming is a waste of time and energy. It does no good. Not to you and not to those you are blaming. And the less time you spend blaming, criticizing and complaining, the more time you will have left to heal yourself, your wounds and your life.

If you continue to blame outside circumstances for the way you feel, and if you continue to put your life in the hands of other people,you will continue to be at the mercy of other people and you will continue to be a victim of your circumstances.

7. <u>Complaining.</u>
"People who never achieve happiness are the ones who complain whenever they're awake, and whenever they're asleep, they are thinking about what to complain about tomorrow.
-Adam Zimbler

Complaining, just like blaming and criticizing, sucks us dry. It keeps us in dark places, and it continues to feed this false idea that our lives will never get better until outside circumstances start to change. But the truth is that it's not the outside world that determines how we feel on the inside, but rather how we feel on the inside that determines how we perceive the outside world.

It's those who feel lost, who have no sense of direction and who can no longer remember what their path in life is who go around projecting their unhappiness into the world.

It's those who have disconnected from their own inner peace and who can no longer feel the abundance of love that flows from their hearts who can't seem to find a way to beat peace with the world around them.

8. <u>Luxury of Criticism.</u>
"When we judge or criticize another person, it says nothing about that person; it merely says something about our own need to be critical."
- Unknown

People grow together with love and appreciation, not blame, judgment and criticism. Relationships flourish when there's respect, understanding and support between the people involved, and they perish when those things are missing. But I didn't know that. I had no idea how relationships were meant to work and how life was me and to be lived.

How we experience the world is largely a projection of who we ourselves are. Our relationships and our lives are nothing but a construct of our thoughts, ideas and beliefs.

Our job is not to criticize what others are doing. Our job is to focus our energy on healing, accepting, loving and embracing all that we are. Because the moment we make peace with ourselves, we also make peace with all those things, people, places and experiences that once caused us to feel hurt, unloved and neglected.

It is only by letting go of the pain we harbor

within us and only by filling our hearts with love and compassion that we can see the world as it really is. Only by loving ourselves can we love the world around us, and only by no longer criticizing ourselves will we stop criticizing others.

9. <u>Living as per others expectations.</u>
"He who trims himself to suit everyone will soon whittle himself away."- Raymond Hull

There's nothing more painful than trying to live your life the way everyone expects you to live it –betraying your own soul just so you can please the world around you.

Too many of us are living a life that is no tour own. Don't let the expectations of others distract you from your own path. Don't put your happiness on hold. Give up living your life according to other people's expectations and start living life in a way that feels right for you instead, even at the risk of "offending" those around you.

Life isn't about pretending. Life isn't about being what others expect you to be and living the way they expect you to live. Life is about being the unique and authentic being you were born to be. It's about walking on the unique and meaningful path you were intended to walk on.

True happiness comes from being yourself, from honoring who you are and from living your life in a unique and authentic way.

10. <u>Self-defeating self-talk.</u>
"We have to learn to be our own best friends because we fall too easily into the trap of being our own worst enemies."- Roderick Thorp

A toxic mind has the power to create a toxic life. It has the power to sabotage our happiness, our relationships and our lives, and it has the power to constantly re-create the same painful experiences, either in the same places with the same people, or with completely different people and incompletely different places.

Thoughts have great power - creative power. With every thought you craft and shape your life. Your present level of self-esteem, your confidence and your sense of self-worth were determined by all the thoughts you have ever thought and all the words you have ever said to yourself.
Take time from your chaotic life to contemplate and to meditate; to familiarize yourself with your innermost thoughts and feelings; to know yourself, to accept yourself and to learn how to love yourself; to empty your mind of all thoughts and to beat peace.

11. <u>Control.</u>
"There as on many people in our society are miserable, sick, and highly stressed is because of an unhealthy attachment to things they have no control over."- Steve Maraboli

Even though things might not always go the way we want them to go, and even though life might not always give us the experiences we want to have, it doesn't mean that life isn't offering us experiences we NEED to have—the experiences that are beneficial for the evolution of our consciousness, the growth of our own soul sand the expansion of our whole beings.

Allow things to unfold naturally without you trying to control everything that happens to you. Allow life to take its natural course, to take you where it needs to take you and not where you think it should take you. Trust that may be life's plans for you are better than your plans.

Let go of fixed plans, rigid beliefs and concepts about how life should unfold, about how things should be, about how people should behave, and keep your mind open to what is.

12. <u>Right to be always right.</u>
"The need to be right – the sign of a vulgar mind."- Albert Camus

Our minds are evolutionarily wired to look out for trouble, and whenever you fall into the trap of arguing with others over who is right and who is wrong, that's exactly what you will find trouble.

When you believe every toxic thought that runs through your mind, being right feels very important because it gives you a false sense of power, security and control. These small victories place you in an imaginary state of superiority, making you feel smarter and more valuable than those you proved wrong.

Fighting over who's right and who's wrong can cause lasting damage to relationships, and to others'
Sense of self-worth. Take a step back and remember what's most important. Don't let your ego get in the way.

13. <u>Need to impress.</u>
"A truly strong person does not need the approval of others any more than a lion needs the approval of sheep."- Vercon Howard

We live in a world that teaches us to look for external love and approval—a world that teaches us that in order for us to feel truly happy, we have to please those around us by behaving in certain ways, and by surrounding ourselves with all kinds of expensive and shiny things.

Your job here on earth is not to spend your life impressing those around you. Your job is to be yourself, authentically and unapologetically, to live your life in a way that makes sense for you—to love yourself and honor yourself more than you care about impressing those around you.

14. <u>Attachment.</u>

In the end these things matter most: How well did you love? How fully did you live? How deeply did you let go? - Buddha

Everything in life changes. Nothing stays the same. And the more you try to cling to things, desperately trying to control and change the natural course of life, the more you will suffer and the unhappier your life will get.

When you hold on too tightly to everything and everyone, when you desperately try to cling to things, people, places and experiences, you take the life out of them and you keep life from taking you where you need to go.

Things, people, and experiences all come and go. Everything changes, nothing remains the same, and the more you resist this truth, the more you try to control the natural course of life by clinging to transitory things, the more complicated your life will get and the more you will continue to suffer.

BENEFITS OF LINGERING EXPERIENCES:

If you want to be happy, have more experiences of happiness and linger on these experiences for the longest period. To get these experiences into our brain we need to train the "gate keeper of our brain".

Any normal day a person passes through many incidents, some positive, some negative and some neutral. The brain always lingers over the negative incidents.

As we passed through centuries and centuries of evolution, our brain has been tuned to remember bad incidents and let go of good incidents. This is for self-preservation and is evident in all species.

This 'Brain Gate keeper" creates Bottle necks in our brain.

All trainers, life coaches, motivators are very good at activating good thoughts. We need to go one step ahead and install these good thoughts in our mind. Make it a way of life.

How do we do it? Imagine your kitchen cabinet. Filled with various items and ingredients. Some healthy (good thoughts) and some unhealthy (bad thoughts).

Now you are cooking. You reach for the ingredients. Try to use more of the healthy items and avoid the unhealthy ones. Initially you will reach for the unhealthy (bad thoughts) but over the time you need to replace them with healthy (good thoughts).

Doing this over and over again your brain will automatically reach for the healthy ingredients (good thoughts) and these will be installed in your brain.

PATH TO HAPPINESS: -

True happiness can emanate from a peaceful mind. It can be true only if it is not dependent on external agents and remains in place irrespective of any fluctuations in our surroundings.

Sometimes Happiness is not achievable due to situations beyond control i.e. losing a family member or close friend, sickness, financial loss etc.

Even in these situations we need to self-realize the situation and accept the loss. This is the only way to overcome the situation. Negative emotions will come up. We need to train our minds to suppress and overcome these thoughts at the earliest.

50% of our happiness comes from how we feel, 40% on our choices and 10% on our circumstances.

Happiness does not mean everything has to be perfect. A good attitude can create happiness. So, it's your choice. It is never late to make happiness a matter of choice.

The next step is to put what you learned into action. Make use of the tips that you found and apply them in your life. So, go ahead and start living the life that you deserve!

You deserve to be happy, so what are you waiting for? Get out there and be happy!

www.ingramcontent.com/pod-product-compliance
Lightning Source LLC
Chambersburg PA
CBHW072000150726
47999CB00001B/501